Editor
Kim Fields

Managing Editor
Mara Ellen Guckian

Illustrator
Mark Mason

Cover Artist
Kevin Barnes

Editor in Chief
Ina Massler Levin, M.A.

Creative Director
Karen J. Goldfluss, M.S. Ed.

Art Coordinator
Renée Christine Yates

Imaging
Craig Gunnell

Publisher

Mary D. Smith, M.S. Ed.

Author

Tracie Heskett, M.Ed.

Teacher Created Resources, Inc.
6421 Industry Way
Westminster, CA 92683
www.teachercreated.com
ISBN: 978-1-4206-2548-6

© 2010 Teacher Created Resources, Inc.
Made in U.S.A.

 # Table of Contents

Introduction

Get ready for *Going Green.* This book will help encourage your students to take care of the environment by adapting the way they live and do things—beginning in the classroom. The students will learn how their daily choices and activities affect the environment. They will discover lifestyle changes that can help preserve the environment. As students gain more knowledge about "Going Green," they will implement the six Rs:

The students will learn to *refuse* excess packaging, *reduce* trash, *reuse* items, and *recycle.* The students will also be encouraged to *research* and learn more about preserving the environment, and to *respond* by sharing their new learning with others.

Becoming more environmentally conscious is important. Many Earth-friendly choices benefit our health and well-being. Learning is the first step in making a positive difference in our world. Topics covered in *Going Green* will allow the students to discover choices they can make at school, which can extend to their home and community.

Although progress has been made in "Going Green" since the first Earth Day in 1970, there is still much to do. The theme of this first global celebration was "Give Earth a Chance." It focused on the purity of air, water, and natural environments. Our society today still faces many environmental dilemmas. To enjoy Earth and its natural resources, we need to work together to take care of our environment. One group of students cannot solve all the problems overnight, but they can do their part. So let's give Earth some help, one child at a time!

How to Use This Book

This book has seven sections, with lessons in each. Each lesson has more than one part. You may want to teach one part each day, with an entire lesson covering approximately a week of class time. Doing so enables you to incorporate these environmental lessons into existing Science or Language Arts curriculum in a busy classroom. The lessons meet cross-curricular standards and include extensions.

The first section includes lessons that help students learn to "Think Green." Encourage your students to try some new things and be willing to experiment. Subsequent sections focus on the Rs of going green: Refuse, Reduce, Reuse, Recycle, and Research. The Respond section helps students make practical applications and extend their learning beyond the classroom.

As you prepare to teach lessons, consider scanning appropriate reproducible pages for use with an interactive whiteboard or photocopying pages to display on an overhead projector. The students may also use individual whiteboards to give responses in class. If the majority of your students have e-mail addresses, send assignments to students via e-mail as appropriate.

Prior to the start of a unit, you may wish to have the students compile magazine pictures or public domain images from the Internet, related to the environment and natural resources, to supplement lessons in this book. The following lessons incorporate pictures: "Processed Foods" (pages 30–32) and "Enriching the Environment" (pages 84–86).

Recycle Magazines Here

| Animals | People | Homes Gardens | Other |

You may also want to preview the vocabulary words listed in the Glossary (pages 92–96). The terms may not be the definitions one might expect; rather, they apply to Going Green. The Glossary can be copied to create student review cards. Simply copy the pages, cut them out, and fold them so that the definitions are on the back. Use glue to stick the front to the back and laminate if appropriate to create a set of vocabulary cards that will last a long time.

Each lesson contains one or more helpful tips for your ELL students. These suggestions may also be appropriate for other students with special needs, or those who just need a little extra assistance.

Setting Up a Green Classroom

Use these ideas as a starting point to brainstorm what will work in your school or district.

Teach by Example

- Use recycled or reusable materials.
- Use a whiteboard and environmentally friendly whiteboard markers instead of handouts.
- Use PowerPoint presentations for lessons.
- Involve students in discussions, rather than written reports, when possible.
- Use an online grading system to reduce paper.
- Turn off computers if away for longer than 30 minutes.
- Teach the students to spoon out or pump small amounts when using soap, hand sanitizer, and glue. Challenge them to use a little dab, not a big squirt!
- Use environmentally friendly cleaning materials and disinfectants. (Combine ¼ cup water and ½ cup vinegar to make a basic disinfectant. Add tea tree essential oil or lemon essential oil if you wish.)
- Teach the students how to use and care for materials so they will last as long as possible.
- Place outlines/worksheets in plastic page protectors so students can write with erasable markers and erase with a rag.
- Share a refrigerator with colleagues.
- Use a mug instead of a paper, plastic, or Styrofoam cup.

A Greener Classroom

- Establish *recycling areas* and a *scrap paper bin*.
- Create an environmentally friendly school supply list and enlist parent help if possible. Here are a few ways to get started:

    —Buy *hand sanitizer* and *liquid soap* in bulk. That way, the pump, which doesn't recycle well, can be reused.

    —Buy *glue* in bulk. Use as small an amount as needed on Styrofoam meat trays, plastic lids, etc.

- Use *recycled cans* to hold classroom supplies including pencils, markers, student name tags, etc.
- Collect the *plastic covers,* (cylinders) that come on containers of 100 CDs. Use these containers to store manipulatives and supplies. They make great planters and water containers, too.
- Make individual *student whiteboards* using shower board (available for purchase at home-improvement stores).
- Use a *non-electric pencil sharpener* and sharpen pencils "the old-fashioned way." This builds muscles, too!
- Use *both sides of paper* (i.e., when writing in a notebook, journal, or on loose-leaf notebook paper).

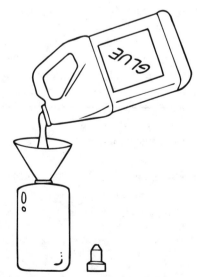

Standards and Benchmarks

Each lesson in *Going Green* meets at least one of the McREL standards and benchmarks, which are used with permission. McREL, Mid-continent Research for Education and Learning, © 2009. Web site: *www.mcrel.org* Telephone: 303-337-0990.

WRITING	Title and Benchmarks
Standard 1. Uses the general skills and strategies of the writing process **Benchmark 1.** Prewriting: Uses a variety of prewriting strategies **Benchmark 2.** Drafting and Revising: Uses a variety of strategies to draft and revise written work **Benchmark 3.** Editing and Publishing: Uses a variety of strategies to edit and publish written work **Benchmark 5.** Uses content, style, and structure appropriate for specific audiences and purposes **Benchmark 6.** Writes expository compositions **Benchmark 8.** Writes compositions about autobiographical incidents **Benchmark 10.** Writes persuasive compositions **Benchmark 11.** Writes compositions that address problems/solutions **Benchmark 12.** Writes in response to literature **Benchmark 13.** Writes business letters and letters of request and response	How to Go Green (1, 2, 3, 5, 10, 12, 13) It's Cool to Go Green (1) Carbon Footprints (2, 6) Environmentally Friendly Practices (2, 6) Processed Foods (8) New Kinds of Plastic (1, 10, 12) The Paperless Debate (1, 2, 3, 10) A Green Lunch (1, 2) Is This Really Trash? (1, 2, 5, 6) The Recycling Process (1, 2, 3, 5) Electronic Landfill (1, 2, 3, 5, 8, 11) Recycle Your Lunch (1) Grow Your Own Lunch (1, 2) Greener Cleaners (11) Green Collar Jobs (1, 2, 3, 5, 13) Conserve Natural Resources (1, 2, 3, 5)
Standard 2. Uses the stylistic and rhetorical aspects of writing **Benchmark 1.** Uses descriptive language that clarifies and enhances ideas (e.g., establishes tone and mood, uses figurative language, uses sensory images and comparisons, uses a thesaurus to choose effective wording) **Benchmark 2.** Uses paragraph form in writing (e.g., arranges sentences in sequential order, uses supporting and follow-up sentences, establishes coherence within and among paragraphs) **Benchmark 3.** Uses a variety of sentence structures to expand and embed ideas (e.g., simple, compound, and complex sentences; parallel structure, such as similar grammatical forms or juxtaposed items) **Benchmark 4.** Uses explicit transitional devices	How to Go Green (1, 2, 3, 4) Carbon Footprints (2) Environmentally Friendly Practices (1, 2, 3, 4) New Kinds of Plastic (2) A Green Lunch (2) The Paperless Debate (1, 2, 3, 4) Electronic Landfill (1, 2, 3, 4) Greener Cleaners (1, 2, 3, 4)
Standard 3. Uses grammatical and mechanical conventions in written compositions **Benchmark 8.** Uses conventions of spelling in written compositions (e.g., spells high-frequency, commonly misspelled words from appropriate grade-level list; uses a dictionary and other resources to spell words; uses common prefixes and suffixes as aids to spelling; applies rules for irregular structural changes) **Benchmark 9.** Uses conventions of capitalization in written compositions (e.g., titles [books, stories, poems, magazines, newspapers, songs, works of art], proper nouns [team names, companies, schools and institutions, departments of government, religions, school subjects], proper adjectives, nationalities, brand names of products) **Benchmark 10.** Uses conventions of punctuation in written compositions (e.g., uses colons, quotation marks, and dashes; uses apostrophes in contractions and possessives, commas with introductory phrases and dependant clauses, semi-colons or a comma and conjunction in compound sentences, commas in a series) **Benchmark 11.** Uses appropriate format in written compositions (e.g., uses italics for titles of books, magazines, plays, movies)	How to Go Green (8, 9, 10, 11) Carbon Footprints (8, 9, 10) Environmentally Friendly Practices (8, 9, 10, 11) The Paperless Debate (8, 9, 10, 11) Electronic Landfill (8, 9, 10, 11) Green Collar Jobs (8, 9, 10, 11) Greener Cleaners (8, 9, 10) Green Collar Jobs (8, 9, 10, 11)
Standard 4. Gathers and uses information for research purposes **Benchmark 3.** Uses a variety of resource materials to gather information for research topics **Benchmark 4.** Determines the appropriateness of an information source for a research topic **Benchmark 5.** Organizes information and ideas from multiple sources in systematic ways **Benchmark 6.** Writes research papers **Benchmark 7.** Uses appropriate methods to cite and document reference sources	It's Cool to Go Green (3, 5) Carbon Footprints (5) Environmentally Friendly Practices (3, 4) New Kinds of Plastic (5) The Paperless Debate (3, 4, 5) The Recycling Process (3, 4, 5) Electronic Landfill (3, 5, 6, 7) Recycle Your Lunch (5) Grow Your Own Lunch (5) Conserve Natural Resources (3, 4, 5) Greener Cleaners (5) Enriching the Environment (3, 4, 5) Green Collar Jobs (3, 4)

 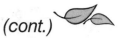

READING	Title and Benchmarks
Standard 5. Uses the general skills and strategies of the reading process **Benchmark 1.** Establishes and adjusts purposes for reading **Benchmark 3.** Uses a variety of strategies to extend reading vocabulary **Benchmark 6.** Reflects on what has been learned after reading and formulates ideas, opinions, and personal responses to texts	How to Go Green (1, 3, 6) It's Cool to Go Green (1) New Kinds of Plastic (1, 3, 6) The Recycling Process (1) Electronic Landfill (1, 3, 6) Recycle Your Lunch (1, 3, 6) Conserve Natural Resources (1, 3) Greener Cleaners (1, 3, 6) Green Collar Jobs (1, 6)
Standard 7. Uses reading skills and strategies to understand and interpret a variety of informational texts **Benchmark 1.** Uses reading skills and strategies to understand a variety of informational texts **Benchmark 3.** Summarizes and paraphrases information in texts **Benchmark 4.** Uses new information to adjust and extend personal knowledge base **Benchmark 5.** Draws conclusions and makes inferences based on explicit and implicit information in texts **Benchmark 6.** Differentiates between fact and opinion in informational texts	How to Go Green (1, 3, 4, 5) It's Cool to Go Green (1, 5) New Kinds of Plastic (4, 6) The Recycling Process (1, 4) Electronic Landfill (1, 3, 4, 5) Recycle Your Lunch (1, 3, 4, 5) Conserve Natural Resources (1, 3, 4, 6) Greener Cleaners (1, 4, 5) Green Collar Jobs (1)

LISTENING AND SPEAKING

Standard 8. Uses listening and speaking strategies for different purposes **Benchmark 1.** Plays a variety of roles in group discussions **Benchmark 2.** Asks questions to seek elaboration and clarification of ideas **Benchmark 3.** Uses strategies to enhance listening comprehension **Benchmark 5.** Uses level-appropriate vocabulary in speech **Benchmark 6.** Makes oral presentations to the class **Benchmark 7.** Uses appropriate verbal and nonverbal techniques for oral presentations **Benchmark 8.** Evaluates strategies used by speakers in oral presentations	How to Go Green (1, 2) It's Cool to Go Green (5, 6) New Kinds of Plastic (1, 2, 3) The Paperless Debate (1, 3, 5, 6, 7, 8) Is This Really Trash? (2) Earth Fashion (1, 6, 7) The Recycling Process (1, 2, 3, 6, 7) Grow Your Own Lunch (1, 6) Conserve Natural Resources (1) Greener Cleaners (6, 7) Green Collar Jobs (3) Enriching the Environment (3, 5, 6, 7)

MEDIA

Standard 9. Uses viewing skills and strategies to understand and interpret visual media **Benchmark 1.** Understands a variety of messages conveyed by visual media **Benchmark 5.** Understands how language choice is used to enhance visual media **Benchmark 6.** Understands how symbols, images, sound, and other conventions are used in visual media **Benchmark 8.** Knows that people with special interests and expectations are the target audience for particular messages or products in visual media; and knows that design, language, and content reflect this	It's Cool to Go Green (1, 5, 6, 8) Processed Foods (1) Is This Really Trash? (8) The Recycling Process (1, 6) Enriching the Environment (1)

SCIENCE

Standard 6. Understands relationships among organisms and their physical environment **Benchmark 2.** Knows factors that affect the number and types of organisms an ecosystem can support **Benchmark 5.** Knows how matter is recycled within ecosystems	Recycle Your Lunch (2, 5) Grow Your Own Lunch (2, 5) Conserve Natural Resources (2)
Standard 8. Understands the structure and properties of matter **Benchmark 8.** Knows that substances react chemically in characteristic ways with other substances to form new substances (compounds) with different characteristic properties **Benchmark 9.** Knows factors that influence reaction rates (e.g., types of substances involved, temperature, concentration of reactant molecules, amount of contact between reactant molecules)	New Kinds of Plastic (8, 9) Recycle Your Lunch (8, 9) Greener Cleaners (8)
Standard 9. Understands the sources and properties of energy **Benchmark 5.** Knows that electrical circuits provide a means of transferring electrical energy to produce heat, light, sound, and chemical changes **Benchmark 6.** Knows that most chemical and nuclear reactions involve a transfer of energy **Benchmark 11.** Understands the origins and environmental impacts of renewable and nonrenewable resources, including energy sources like fossil fuels	Carbon Footprints (11) The Paperless Debate (5, 6, 11) Electronic Landfill (5) Conserve Natural Resources (11)

SCIENCE *(cont.)*	Title and Benchmarks
Standard 11. Understands the nature of scientific knowledge **Benchmark 1.** Understands the nature of scientific explanations **Benchmark 2.** Knows that all scientific ideas are tentative and subject to change and improvement in principle, but for most core ideas in science, there is much experimental and observational confirmation **Benchmark 4.** Knows that models are often used to think about things that cannot be observed or investigated directly	Processed Food (4) New Kinds of Plastic (1) The Recycling Process (4) Greener Cleaners (2)
Standard 12. Understands the nature of scientific inquiry **Benchmark 7.** Establishes relationships based on evidence and logical argument	Carbon Footprints (7) Conserve Natural Resources (7) Greener Cleaners (7)
Standard 13. Understands the scientific enterprise **Benchmark 1.** Knows that people of all backgrounds and with diverse interests, talents, qualities, and motivations engage in fields of science and engineering; some of these people work in teams and others work alone, but all communicate extensively with others **Benchmark 2.** Knows that the work of science requires a variety of human abilities, qualities, and habits of mind **Benchmark 3.** Knows various settings in which scientists and engineers may work **Benchmark 6.** Knows ways in which science and society influence one another	Green Collar Jobs (1, 2, 3, 6)
GEOGRAPHY	
Standard 7. Knows the physical processes that shape patterns on Earth's surface **Benchmark 2.** Knows the processes that produce renewable and nonrenewable resources	Carbon Footprints (2)
Standard 8. Understands the characteristics of ecosystems on Earth's surface **Benchmark 5.** Knows the potential impact of human activities within a given ecosystem on the carbon, nitrogen, and oxygen cycles	Carbon Footprints (5) New Kinds of Plastic (5) Recycle Your Lunch (5) Conserve Natural Resources (5)
Standard 14. Understands how human actions modify the physical environment **Benchmark 1.** Understands the environmental consequences of people changing the physical environment **Benchmark 3.** Understands the ways in which technology influences the human capacity to modify the physical environment **Benchmark 4.** Understands the environmental consequences of both the unintended and intended outcomes of major technological changes in human history	How to Go Green (1) Carbon Footprints (1, 4) Environmentally Friendly Practices (4) New Kinds of Plastic (1, 3, 4) A Green Lunch (3) The Paperless Debate (3) Is This Really Trash? (1) Electronic Landfill (1, 3, 4) Conserve Natural Resources (1, 3, 4) Greener Cleaners (1)
Standard 16. Understands the changes that occur in the meaning, use, distribution, and importance of resources **Benchmark 1.** Understands the reasons for conflicting viewpoints regarding how resources should be used **Benchmark 2.** Knows strategies for wise management and use of renewable, flow, and nonrenewable resources **Benchmark 5.** Understands the role of technology in resource acquisition and use, and its impact on the environment	How to Go Green (2) It's Cool to Go Green (2) Carbon Footprints (1, 2) Environmentally Friendly Practices (2) New Kinds of Plastic (1, 2) The Paperless Debate (1, 5) Is This Really Trash? (2) Earth Fashion (2) The Recycling Process (2) Electronic Landfill (2) Grow Your Own Lunch (2) Conserve Natural Resources (1, 2, 5)
Standard 18. Understands global development and environmental issues **Benchmark 1.** Understands how the interaction between physical and human systems affects current conditions on Earth	Carbon Footprints (1) Enriching the Environment (1)
SOCIAL STUDIES	
Standard 1. Understands that group and cultural influences contribute to human development, identity, and behavior **Benchmark 4.** Understands that technology, especially in transportation and communication, is increasingly important in spreading ideas, values, and behavior patterns within a society and among different societies **Benchmark 5.** Understands that various factors affect decisions that individuals make	It's Cool to Go Green (4, 5) Processed Foods (5) Earth Fashion (5) Electronic Landfill (4, 5) Grow Your Own Lunch (5) Green Collar Jobs (4, 5)

SOCIAL STUDIES (cont.)	Title and Benchmarks
Standard 2. Understands various meanings of social group, general implications of group membership, and different ways that groups function **Benchmark 6.** Understands how language, literature, the arts, architecture, other artifacts, traditions, beliefs, values, and behaviors contribute to the development and transmission of culture	It's Cool to Go Green (6) Earth Fashion (6)
Standard 4. Understands conflict, cooperation, and interdependence among individuals, groups, and institutions **Benchmark 2.** Understands that most groups have formal or informal procedures for arbitrating disputes among their members **Benchmark 5.** Understands how tensions might arise between expressions of individuality and group or institutional efforts to promote social conformity	New Kinds of Plastic (5) The Paperless Debate (2)
HEALTH	
Standard 2. Knows environmental and external factors that affect individual and community health **Benchmark 2.** Understands how various messages from the media, peers, and other sources impact health practices **Benchmark 3.** Knows local, state, federal, and international efforts to contain an environmental crisis and prevent a recurrence	Carbon Footprints (3) Processed Foods (2) A Green Lunch (2)
Standard 7. Knows how to maintain and promote personal health **Benchmark 3.** Knows strategies and skills that are used to attain personal health goals **Benchmark 4.** Understands how changing information, abilities, priorities, and responsibilities influence personal health goals	Processed Foods (3, 4) A Green Lunch (3, 4) Grow Your Own Lunch (3)
MATH	
Standard 6. Understands and applies basic and advanced concepts of statistics and data analysis **Benchmark 4.** Reads and interprets data in charts, tables, and plots **Benchmark 5.** Uses data and statistical measures for a variety of purposes **Benchmark 6.** Organizes and displays data using tables, graphs, frequency distributions, and plots	The Paperless Debate (4, 5, 6) A Green Lunch (4, 5, 6)
VISUAL ARTS	
Standard 1. Understands and applies media, techniques, and processes related to the visual arts **Benchmark 2.** Knows how the qualities and characteristics of art media, techniques, and processes can be used to enhance communication of experiences and ideas	The Recycling Process (2) Conserve Our Natural Resources (2)
THEATER	
Standard 2. Uses acting skills **Benchmark 2.** Uses basic acting skills to develop characterizations that suggest artistic choices **Benchmark 4.** Interacts as an invented character in improvised and scripted scenes	It's Cool to Go Green (2, 4) Is This Really Trash? (4)

Date: _____

Dear Parent or Guardian,

This year we are learning how to Go Green and make choices that help our environment. Adopting environmentally friendly behaviors involves new ways of thinking.

The students will focus on how they can make environmentally friendly choices as a class and as individuals to become more Green. They will learn to refuse excess packaging, reduce trash, reuse items, and recycle. The students will also be encouraged to research and learn more about preserving the environment, and to respond by sharing their new learning with others.

Scientists have raised awareness and concerns about environmental issues, such as nonrenewable energy sources, the negative effects of using fossil fuels on the atmosphere and climate, and the harmful effects of pollution on plant and animal life. To enjoy Earth and its natural resources, we need to learn to work together to take care of our environment.

One group of students cannot solve all the problems overnight, but they can do their part. Similarly, we do not expect one family to be able to incorporate all the ideas and suggestions that students discuss in class. We hope that you will talk with your child about what he or she is learning, and will support your child in any environmental practices he or she would like to try outside of class. We hope you will also consider *one way* in which you can Go Green along with your student.

Thank you,

_____

How to Go Green

Objective: Given the six "R" words of environmentally friendly behavior, the students will examine examples of others who are Going Green and report back to the class.

Vocabulary

- refuse
- reduce
- reuse
- recycle
- research
- respond

Materials

- Learn the Rs on pages 13–14
- Going Green Case Studies on pages 15–16
- index card for each student (eco-friendlier option: individual student whiteboards, the class blog, or e-mail)
- cardboard shoe box with lid
- scissors
- cardstock or poster board, and appropriate marker (optional)

Preparation

1. Prepare a large word card for each "R" word (*Refuse, Reduce, Reuse, Recycle, Research, Respond*) if desired, using cardstock or poster board and a marker.
2. Prepare a shoe box as a "suggestion box" by cutting a slit in the lid.
3. Copy one Going Green Case Study for each group of students.

Opening

1. Ask the students, "What does it mean to Go Green?"
2. Have the students activate their prior knowledge by writing their responses to the question on index cards, whiteboards, or by posting ideas on the class blog. If time allows, the students may share their responses with partners. If responses are done on index cards, consider creating a chart and placing each index card under the appropriate "R" word heading.
3. Invite several students to share their responses to the opening question with the class. As the students share responses related to a specific "R" word, mention the word and write it on the board or show a prepared word card. Introduce any "R" words not previously mentioned. Refer to Learn the Rs to review definitions and concepts for the "R" words.

Note to Teacher:
The Going Green Case Studies have the following reading levels: Hopeville (7.2), Meriden (4.4), Springfield (7.0), and Oak Ridge (6.3).

 # How to Go Green *(cont.)*

Part 1

1. Divide the students into groups of four students each. Assign or suggest group roles if desired:

    - Reader
    - Scribe (takes notes)
    - Task Manager (ensures all members of the group participate and stay on task)
    - Idea Coordinator (matches "R" words to specific actions)

Note: If a group has more than four students, have two students share the task of reading.

2. Distribute a different case study to each group. Each group will read and discuss the case study.

Part 2

1. Direct the students to take notes on how each school in their assigned case study (or classroom) practices the "R" words.
2. Have the students identify ways they can put the "R" words into practice in their own classroom.
3. Encourage the students to expand on the ideas presented in the case study and come up with new ideas that apply to their classroom or school.

Closing

1. Have the students write new or revised suggestions for Going Green in your classroom on index cards and put the cards in the prepared suggestion box.
2. Review the vocabulary words by reading one suggestion at a time. As a class, decide to which "R" word category the suggestion relates.
3. As a whole group, decide on a few suggestions to implement. If time allows, the students may post suggestions on a class blog or Web page.

Extension

Have the students write and submit a more formal plan or proposal for Going Green in your classroom. Suggest that the students use the format of a business letter, memo, or proposal.

ELL Tip

Work with a small group to discuss how a specific suggestion relates to one of the "R" word concepts.

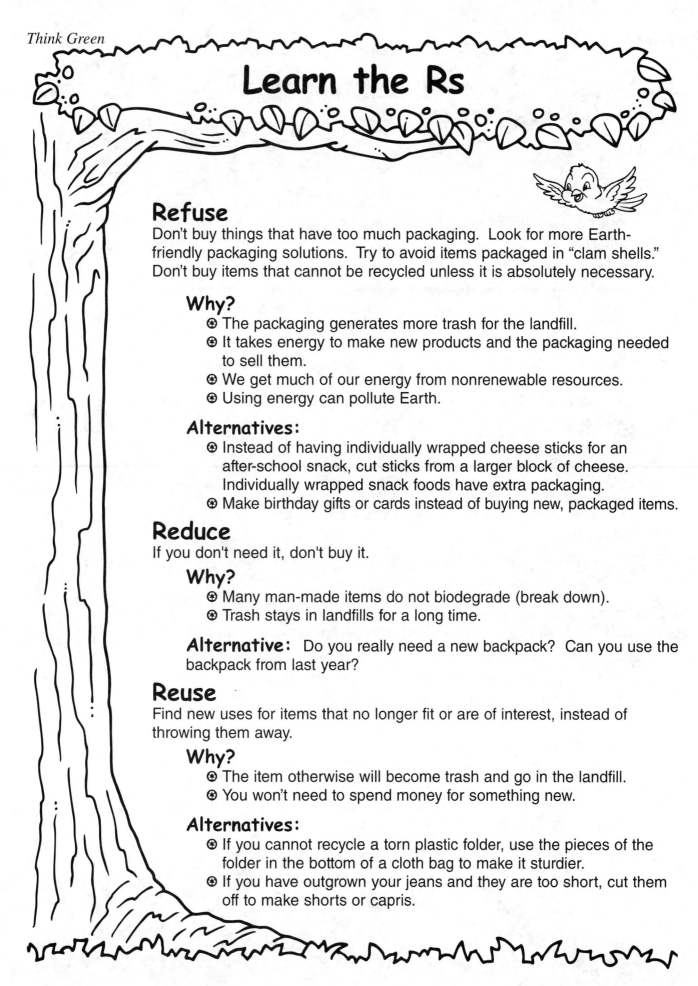

Learn the Rs

Refuse

Don't buy things that have too much packaging. Look for more Earth-friendly packaging solutions. Try to avoid items packaged in "clam shells." Don't buy items that cannot be recycled unless it is absolutely necessary.

Why?

- ✪ The packaging generates more trash for the landfill.
- ✪ It takes energy to make new products and the packaging needed to sell them.
- ✪ We get much of our energy from nonrenewable resources.
- ✪ Using energy can pollute Earth.

Alternatives:

- ✪ Instead of having individually wrapped cheese sticks for an after-school snack, cut sticks from a larger block of cheese. Individually wrapped snack foods have extra packaging.
- ✪ Make birthday gifts or cards instead of buying new, packaged items.

Reduce

If you don't need it, don't buy it.

Why?

- ✪ Many man-made items do not biodegrade (break down).
- ✪ Trash stays in landfills for a long time.

Alternative: Do you really need a new backpack? Can you use the backpack from last year?

Reuse

Find new uses for items that no longer fit or are of interest, instead of throwing them away.

Why?

- ✪ The item otherwise will become trash and go in the landfill.
- ✪ You won't need to spend money for something new.

Alternatives:

- ✪ If you cannot recycle a torn plastic folder, use the pieces of the folder in the bottom of a cloth bag to make it sturdier.
- ✪ If you have outgrown your jeans and they are too short, cut them off to make shorts or capris.

Learn the Rs

Recycle

Sort bottles, cans, paper, plastic, etc., and recycle to convert them, rather than fill a landfill.

Why?

⊕ Making new items requires huge amounts of energy (electricity).
⊕ Recycling takes less energy and uses fewer resources.

Alternatives:

⊕ Recycle plastic milk jugs. They can be made into park benches and playground equipment.
⊕ Recycle paper. It might be used to make the next book you read.

Research

Learn more about environmentally friendly products.

Why?

⊕ Be part of the solution, not part of the problem.
⊕ Support companies that want to take care of the environment.
⊕ Learn how to take better care of Earth.

Alternative: Use the Internet or the library to learn about Earth-friendly packaging.

Respond

Share with others what you have learned about helping the environment.

Why?

⊕ More people can do environmentally friendly things.
⊕ More people can purchase items with environmentally friendly packaging.

Alternatives:

⊕ I can tell my parents what I learn about recycling, and help recycle things at home.
⊕ I can remind my friends not to litter or waste water.
⊕ I can remind others to turn off lights.

14

 # How to Go Green *(cont.)*

Going Green Case Studies

Hopeville, New York

The Owen D. Olds School has solar panels and a nature preserve. The solar panels generate electricity for a few classrooms.

Every classroom and office has recycling containers for paper and plastic. The school also recycles computer monitors and ink and toner cartridges.

The nature preserve includes trails, caves, and waterfalls. Each spring, trout are released into one of the streams. Students planted more than 200 trees one summer. They maintain birdhouses throughout the preserve.

Students in the "Learn and Serve" Club plant a garden each year. They raise vegetables and donate the produce to a local food pantry.

Meriden, South Dakota

This school has a classroom with insulated windows. They think the classroom will not need electric heat until later in the school year. The sun will heat the room.

The school has a new heat pump that uses electricity. The lights turn off when people leave the room.

Students wear gloves to pick up litter on a community street one day a week after school.

How to Go Green (cont.)

Going Green Case Studies (cont.)

Springfield, Missouri

Fourth-grade students at Greenwillow School use rags instead of paper towels to clean up around the classroom. They use old (but clean) white socks to erase whiteboards. The classroom has fluorescent light bulbs.

Students and teachers recycle paper. Paper that is printed on only one side is reused and then recycled. The fourth-graders reuse plastic containers and tin cans for art projects and storage. Teachers use cardboard boxes for storage in the classroom. Teachers reuse plastic bags to send homework to absent students.

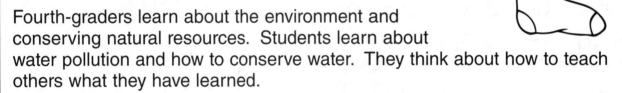

Fourth-graders learn about the environment and conserving natural resources. Students learn about water pollution and how to conserve water. They think about how to teach others what they have learned.

Students use reusable containers in their lunches. They have personal water bottles that they refill instead of buying bottled water.

Oak Ridge, Colorado

Passages Charter School has a solar panel system. Students study energy use and suggest ways to conserve it.

Students compost leftovers from lunch. Students researched what they should include to get the best results. They also learned about soil composition. The school will sell compost to the community.

Many teachers walk or ride bikes to school. The school uses biodegradable cleaning products.

It's Cool to Go Green

Objective: Given articles to read, the students will identify current trends and reasons to Go Green and create a commercial to inform others.

Vocabulary

- trend
- impact
- media

Materials

- dictionary (or Glossary pages 92–96) for each student or pair of students
- newspaper and magazine articles
- compiled list of Web sites (see Technology Resources on pages 89–91)
- word processing software
- music, materials for visual aids, or props as needed for student presentations (optional)
- audiovisual recording equipment (optional)

Preparation

1. Have the students bring newspaper and magazine articles to class on the topic of Going Green. **Note:** This should be done at least one week prior to the activity.
2. See Technology Resources to get started. Compile blogs or Web site URLs into a document. This will allow the students to remain focused on relevant Web sites; they need not search the Internet but rather will directly access content you want them to view.

Opening

1. On the board, write the vocabulary words: *trend, impact,* and *media*. Have the students look up each word and write the definition in their own words.
2. Pair each student with a partner. They will give a "real story" example to their partner to demonstrate what each word means. For example, a student could say he and his friends have a positive *impact* on the environment when they participate in home or classroom recycling.
3. Refer to the Glossary on pages 92–96 to clarify the meanings of vocabulary words as necessary.

 # It's Cool to Go Green *(cont.)*

Part 1

1. Ask the students why it might be "cool" to Go Green. Conduct a class discussion about trends in student behavior related to the environment. For example, the students might identify a *trend* among their friends to wear used jeans. Introduce the collection of articles and other resources.

2. If there are not enough magazine or newspaper articles for each student to have his or her own, invite the students to share and trade as time permits.

3. Have the students research and read at least one article or Web site about a current trend in behavior that impacts the environment in a positive way. Direct the students to take notes as they read.

4. Ask the students what they learned from the *media* about current trends in environmentally friendly behaviors.

Part 2

1. Divide the students into groups with three to five students in each group.

2. Have the students share what they learned about different ways people help the environment.

3. Instruct each group to prepare a "commercial" and present it to the class. The students may use music, visual aids, or props.

Closing

1. Have the students present their commercials to the class.

2. Use a class discussion about the student presentations to review the vocabulary words: *trend, impact, media.*

3. Ask the students which behaviors depicted in the presentations are trends and why.

4. Discuss how the *media* can have an *impact* on how people act.

Extension

Record the students' presentations to broadcast to others in the school if audiovisual (multi-media) recording equipment is available. Or have the students present their commercials live at a school assembly to inform and increase awareness about environmentally friendly behavior.

ELL Tip

Use sentence frames to help the students tell a "real story" during the Opening vocabulary exercise.

One trend I have seen among many of my friends that helps the environment

is _____.

I can have a positive impact on the environment by _____.

I can learn _____ from the media.

Carbon Footprints

Objective: Given a sample of major environmental events, the students will construct a time line depicting significant events related to "carbon footprints" on Earth and then create their own carbon footprint time line.

Vocabulary

- chronological
- carbon footprint
- carbon dioxide

1969 NEPA—National Environmental Policy Act (positive)

1990 National Environmental Education Act (positive)

Materials

- Environmental Events strips on pages 22–23
- bulletin board and staples or push pins
- butcher paper or other scrap paper for student time lines
- scissors
- tape
- cardstock
- access to an interactive whiteboard, slide presentation software, one computer station for each team (optional)

2010 40th Anniversary of Earth Day (positive)

Preparation

1. Photocopy the Environmental Events strips onto cardstock and cut them apart. Make one set for each team.

2. If using butcher paper for student time lines, cut one 36" piece for each pair of students. Cut each piece in half lengthwise to create a narrower strip for each student.

3. If using other paper, the students will tape two or three strips together lengthwise to form a 36" time line.

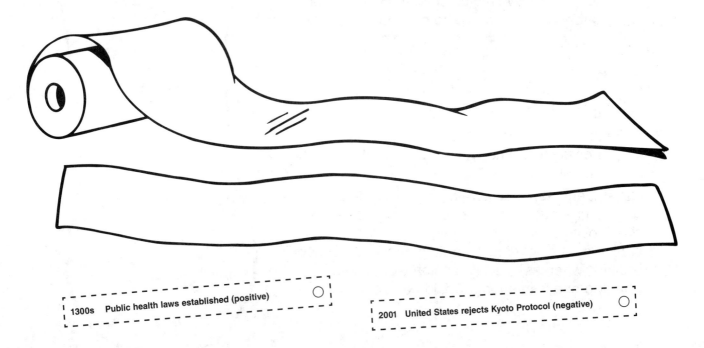

1300s Public health laws established (positive)

2001 United States rejects Kyoto Protocol (negative)

Carbon Footprints *(cont.)*

Opening

1. Introduce the new vocabulary, *chronological, carbon footprint*, and *carbon dioxide*, and review the word *impact*. Ask two students to stand in front of the room and face the class. Write the word *impact* on the board behind them. Call on students randomly to give clues to the students in front to help them guess the vocabulary word.

2. Have a different pair of students stand in front. Write the word *chronological* on the board. Ask the class to give clues for the students to guess the vocabulary word.

3. Discuss the meaning of the term, *carbon footprint*, with the class. Explain that this term refers to the demand human activity places on Earth's ecosystems.

4. Explain that a small footprint might be a person who recycles—compared to the larger footprint of an amusement park, which uses a considerable amount of electricity.

5. Share with the class the following facts about *carbon dioxide:*

   - Carbon dioxide is a natural gas consisting of carbon and oxygen.
   - People and animals breathe carbon dioxide out, and plants absorb the gas during the day.
   - Oceans and growing plants remove carbon dioxide from the atmosphere.
   - Human activities, such as burning fossil fuels (coal, oil, natural gas) and deforestation, result in greater increases of carbon dioxide emissions into the atmosphere.

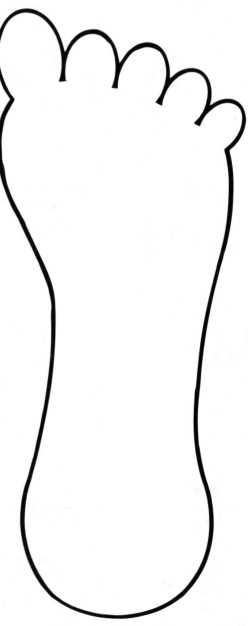

Part 1

1. Continue discussing the idea of a carbon footprint. A smaller footprint would be created by a recycler, and a larger footprint would be created by a polluter. A *carbon footprint* measurement compares the human demand for resources with Earth's ability to regenerate or replenish those resources. The demand for resources, compared to Earth's supply, is not in balance.

2. Invite the students to think of things people do that have a positive or a negative impact on the environment.

3. List student responses on the board in a two-column chart using different colors (e.g., green or blue, positive; black or red, negative). For example, turning off the lights when exiting a room would be positive, whereas, leaving the lights on all day when no one is in a room would be negative.

 # Carbon Footprints *(cont.)*

Part 2

1. Divide the students into two or more teams. Distribute one set of Environmental Events strips to each team. *Optional:* The students may work together as a class, taking turns using an interactive whiteboard.

2. Have the students place the strips in *chronological* order to construct a Carbon Footprint time line. If using slide presentation software, the students will enter the information from each card to create a slide and manipulate the slides into the proper order. If the students know approximate dates corresponding to any items listed during Part 1, they may add those events to their time line as well.

3. Consider having the students color the time line dots in corresponding colors to indicate positive and negative influences on the environment on the time line. Or have the students draw a small (green) carbon footprint next to positive environmental events and a large (black or red) footprint next to negative events.

4. Ask the students to state how and why each event reduces or increases society's carbon footprint.

Closing

1. Call on two or three students to give a brief explanation of *carbon footprints* and how they have an *impact* on Earth.

2. Have the students write a paragraph describing ways people can reduce their carbon footprints.

3. Ask the students to list ways in which they have impacted the environment (positive or negative). They may cut out footprint shapes like the one on page 20 and color-code each item to show a beneficial or non-beneficial environmental effect.

Extension

Have the students research one of the events on the Carbon Footprint time line to add more information.

Have native speakers assist you in compiling pictures to accompany events on the Environmental Events time line. Use the pictures to explain and describe each event.

 # Environmental Events

1300s   Public health laws established (positive)   ◯

1300s   Sanitary laws regulating disposal of garbage initiated (positive)   ◯

1500s   Industrialization leads to deforestation and burning more coal instead of wood in England (negative)   ◯

1690   Governor of Pennsylvania requires one acre of trees preserved for every five acres cleared (positive)   ◯

1700s   Disagreements over waste disposal, water pollution, and industrial enterprises in the United States (negative)   ◯

1800s   U.S. citizens, scientists, numerous organizations, and lawmakers come together to support wildlife (positive)   ◯

1905   London meeting expresses concern about air pollution (positive)   ◯

1916   Congress establishes the National Park Service (positive)   ◯

1920s   High use of lead found in United States (negative)   ◯

1928   First warnings of damage to atmosphere published (positive)   ◯

1940s–1960s   Industrial pesticides that included DDT were produced by the United States to control diseases such as typhus and malaria (negative)   ◯

1969   NEPA—National Environmental Policy Act (positive)   ◯

1970   Earth Day initiated in the United States (positive)   ◯

1970   U.S. Environmental Protection Agency established Clean Air Act (positive)   ◯

 # Environmental Events (cont.)

1974	Scientists first suggested that man-made chlorofluorocarbons (CFCs) might cause ozone depletion	◯
1986	Chernobyl—world's worst nuclear power accident (negative)	◯
1989	Exxon Valdez—largest oil spill in U.S. history (negative)	◯
1990	National Environmental Education Act (positive)	◯
1992	William Rees created term *ecological footprint* to raise awareness (positive)	◯
1997	Kyoto Protocol, Japan—amendment to United Nations Framework Convention on Climate Change (UNFCCC); countries that sign agreement commit to reduce carbon dioxide emissions and other greenhouse gases (positive)	◯
2000–2008	Carbon emissions increased by 3.5% per year in spite of increased awareness regarding potential climate change (negative)	◯
2001	United States rejects Kyoto Protocol (negative)	◯
2005	Arctic Council reports that the Arctic region has warmed twice as fast as the rest of the world over the past 50 years (negative)	◯
2008	No Child Left Inside Act for environmental education (positive)	◯
2008	Coal sludge spill in Tennessee is larger than the Valdez oil spill—the sludge contained concentrated levels of mercury and arsenic (negative)	◯
2009	U.S. Department of Energy Solar Decathlon with 800 students from four countries participating in demonstrations of solar housing (positive)	◯
2010	40th Anniversary of Earth Day (positive)	◯

Environmentally Friendly Practices

Objective: Given recycling symbols and images of products, the students will identify examples of products that follow environmentally friendly practices and express the importance of these practices in writing.

Vocabulary

- consumer
- efficient
- fiber
- organic
- post-consumer
- pre-consumer
- sustainable
- synthetic
- waste

Materials

- Recycling Reference sheet on page 29
- Recycling Symbol Cards on pages 27–28 (eco-friendlier option: scan into interactive whiteboard)
- age-appropriate magazines and newspapers, particularly advertisements or public domain online images
- examples of products with recycling symbols or pictures of products with recycling symbols
- interactive whiteboard or access to word processing or slide presentation software
- scanner
- glue and scissors (optional)
- white paper or poster board and scrap paper or index cards (optional)

Recycling Reference

Plastic Item	Marked	Can Be Made Into
Soda bottles, food product packaging, oven-ready meal trays, and vitamin bottles	1 PETE	Soda bottles, paint brushes, carpeting, microfleece for clothing and blankets; fiber filling for sleeping bags, comforters, coats, and vests
Milk, juice, and water jugs; shampoo, detergent, and other cleaning fluid bottles	2 HDPE	Milk, juice, and water jugs; drainage pipes; trash cans; and the fibers used in bullet-proof vests
Clear food wrap, cooking oil bottles, and molded plastic lawn chairs	3 PVC	Recyclable plastics marked 3–7 are mixed together and used to make big plastic items such as:
Rings for 6-packs, coffee can lids, grocery store bags, and trash can liners	4 LDPE	• picnic tables
		• sand boxes
Margarine and whipped topping tubs, yogurt cups, snap-on lids, and microwaveable meal trays	5 PP	• plumbing pipes
		• fencing
		• park benches
Styrofoam meat trays, egg cartons, and cups; insulation; plastic forks, spoons, and knives; and packing "peanuts"	6 PS	• playground equipment
		• plastic lumber
		• lawn chairs
Squeeze bottles for jellies, sauces, and syrups; and various other plastics	7 Other	• storage bins

Preparation

1. Have the students collect pictures of various products that might include a recycling symbol on the packaging. Examples include cereal boxes, packages of binder paper or computer paper, packages of paper napkins, plastic juice or water bottles, milk jugs, yogurt containers, CD jackets, packages of pencils (paperboard symbol and possibly "does not contain rainforest wood" logo), glue bottles, and printer ink cartridge boxes (possibly two symbols, one for recycling the cardboard box and one with information about recycling the ink cartridges).

2. If desired, scan Recycling Symbols into the interactive whiteboard, or a word processing or slide presentation document. If not, make one copy for display and additional copies for the students.

3. Briefly review the Recycling Reference sheet prior to the lesson.

Environmentally Friendly Practices (cont.)

Opening

1. Assign student partners the following word pairs (more than one pair of students will have each word pair).

   - post-consumer—pre-consumer
   - waste—efficient
   - organic—synthetic

2. Each partner will look up a different word.

3. Have the students compare their words and answer these questions:

   —How are the two words similar?

   —In what ways do the words have different meanings?

4. Introduce the additional vocabulary words, *sustainable* and *fiber*. Discuss with the students what it means to be *sustainable* (resources that can continue to be used). Tell the students that the word *fiber* means a long, thin thread of material such as cotton, wool, hemp, or nylon.

Part 1

1. Display a copy of the Recycling Symbols cards.

2. Review each symbol with the class, asking the students if they have seen the symbol before and where they have noticed it.

3. Ask the students on what products they might expect to see each symbol. Encourage the students to think of specific products. For example, computer paper might have the *% of recycled material* symbol or a small electrical appliance might display the *Energy Star* symbol.

4. Encourage the students to be on the lookout for recycling symbols and continue to report sightings of symbols they see outside of school.

Part 2

1. If using an interactive whiteboard or other computer software, have the students download images or scan pictures of products.

2. Direct the students to use drag-and-drop features to match each recycling symbol to one or more specific products that might display the symbol on the packaging.

3. If computer technology is unavailable, distribute copies of the Recycling Symbols to each student or pair of students. Have the students cut apart the recycling symbols to make cards.

4. Ask the students to cut out pictures of specific products and match them to various recycling symbols. If they have spotted symbols on items in stores, they can draw pictures of them or write the names of the items on scrap paper or index cards.

5. The students may glue pictures and symbols to paper or poster board to create a visual reminder of environmentally friendly products.

Environmentally Friendly Practices (cont.)

Closing

1. Have the students write a one-page essay describing the importance of the environmental practices represented by the symbols.

2. Encourage the students to use as many vocabulary words as possible in their essays.

3. If appropriate, have interested students do additional research using available resources.

Extension

Have the students conduct a "scavenger hunt" in which they visit local stores and locate various recycling symbols used on packaging. The students should sketch each symbol they find and write a brief (one or more words) description of the product on which they saw the symbol.

ELL Tip

For the Closing activity, allow the students to write a simple one-paragraph essay, focusing on one recycling symbol and the related environmental practices. Review the symbols with a small group of students to scaffold them as they begin to plan and write their essays.

Environmentally Friendly Practices *(cont.)*

Recycling Symbol Cards

Product labels that read "environmentally safe," "Earth-friendly," or "natural" are not specific enough. A picture of Earth or a green package also does not give adequate information. Read labels to find out if a product is good for the environment. Items with the following symbols are better for our environment.

Directions: Cut out these symbols and enlarge as needed to create flashcards or a display.

♲	This symbol means an item can and should be recycled. This does not mean it will be recycled. Not all community recycling programs have the ability to recycle all recyclable materials (e.g., plastics).
♻	___% recycled material This symbol means that an item is made from a certain percentage of recycled items.
100% Post Consumer Waste • 100% Post Consumer Waste	____% recycled fibers This symbol means it has paper or cloth in it that is made from recycled materials.

Environmentally Friendly Practices *(cont.)*

Recycling Symbols Cards *(cont.)*

Directions: Cut out these symbols and enlarge as needed to create flashcards or a display.

1 PETE

2 HDPE

3 PVC

4 LDPE

5 PP

6 PS

7 Other

28

 # Recycling Reference

Plastic Item	Marked	Can Be Made Into
Soda bottles, food product packaging, oven-ready meal trays, and vitamin bottles	1 PETE	Soda bottles; paint brushes; carpeting; microfleece for clothing and blankets; fiber filling for sleeping bags, comforters, coats, and vests
Milk, juice, and water jugs; shampoo, detergent, and other cleaning fluid bottles	2 HDPE	Milk, juice, and water jugs; drainage pipes; trash cans; fibers used in bullet-proof vests
Clear food wrap, cooking oil bottles, and molded plastic lawn chairs	3 PVC	Recyclable plastics marked 3–7 are mixed together and used to make big plastic items such as: • picnic tables • sandboxes • plumbing pipes • fencing • park benches • playground equipment • plastic lumber • lawn chairs • storage bins
Rings for 6-packs, coffee can lids, grocery store bags, and trash can liners	4 LDPE	
Margarine and whipped topping tubs, yogurt cups, snap-on lids, and microwaveable meal trays	5 PP	
Styrofoam meat trays, egg cartons, and cups; insulation; plastic forks, spoons, and knives; and packing "peanuts"	6 PS	
Squeeze bottles for jellies, sauces, and syrups; and various other plastics	7 Other	

Processed Foods

Objective

Given sample nutrition labels, the students will learn to read labels to identify ingredients and additives in foods.

Vocabulary

- processed
- ingredient
- additive

Materials

- Play Dough recipe on page 32
- food coloring
- play dough toys or kitchen utensils
- apple and apple products with nutritional labels (e.g., jar of organic applesauce, regular applesauce, apple energy bar)
- sample ingredient labels from common lunch or snack food items
- overhead projector or interactive whiteboard (optional)
- magazine pictures (optional)

Preparation

1. Gather an apple and apple products.
2. Download nutritional information for each product or gather labels to present to students on an overhead projector or interactive whiteboard. Or enlarge copies to post in the room for viewing in smaller groups.
3. Prepare play dough, but do not add the coloring.

Opening

1. Conduct a demonstration with homemade play dough. Tell the students to pretend it is a food.
2. Add food coloring to the dough. Ask the class how the "food" has changed.
3. "Process" the dough using play dough toys and kitchen utensils to cut and shape the dough. Ask the students once again how it has changed.
4. Ask the class if anyone knows a word to describe what you have done to the dough. (processed it using an additive) You have *processed* the dough, or used a series of steps to change it and added a new ingredient.
5. Explain that food can also be *processed*. Much of the food we eat goes through steps to prepare it, and sometimes change it, before we eat the food. Cooking is a way of processing some foods.
7. Write the following sentences with blanks on the board. Invite the students to guess which words might complete the sentences. Post the vocabulary words if necessary.

   Processed foods have many <u>ingredients</u>. <u>Additives</u> are extra things that are added to food.
8. Ask the students what the difference is between an *ingredient* and an *additive*. (An *ingredient* is one of the things an item is made from; an *additive* is something that is added to a substance to change it in some way. Additives can be used to sweeten a product, make it last longer, or to make it look more appealing.)

 # Processed Foods *(cont.)*

Part 1

1. Ask the students to give examples of how food is processed (applesauce—*apples are cooked, which changes the consistency*; milk—*pasteurized to kill bacteria and make it safer to drink;* meat—*is often cooked*).

2. Display the apple and samples of apple products with ingredient labels.

3. Invite the students to compare the different products. Discuss how the main ingredient in each food item is apples. Some of the items have other ingredients as well.

4. Explain that we can learn to read ingredient labels to see what is really in the food we eat. Then we can decide if it is something we want to eat. If you do not recognize or cannot pronounce an ingredient, you might want to think twice about eating it.

Part 2

1. Display sample ingredient labels from common lunch or snack food items.

2. Work with the class to create a T-chart. Compare ingredients they recognize and those they do not. Or compare food items with ingredients that are additives. For example, a package of crackers might list wheat and oil as food ingredients, and BHT as an additive added to the packaging to preserve freshness.

3. Periodically have the students create new T-charts for food items to examine the ingredients and/or additives. Encourage discussions about the nutritional value of different foods. Which foods do we need to eat to be healthy? Which ones do we eat strictly for enjoyment? Why is it important to strike a balance?

Part 3

1. Explain that some things we do to our food are good things that make sense. These steps do not harm us or the environment. For instance, we peel a banana or an orange before we eat it. We crack an egg and cook it.

2. We freeze vegetables to preserve vitamins and keep them as fresh as possible for longer periods of time. Canned foods give us access to fruits or vegetables even when they are not in season.

3. Tell the students that some foods go through many more steps in a factory before we eat them. Often *processed* foods have extra sugar, salt, or fat added to them. Extra ingredients may be added for taste such as sugar added to whole wheat cereal. Some ingredients, such as salt, are added to food to help preserve it.

4. Processed foods are easy to heat and eat quickly. Astronauts, campers, and people in emergency situations benefit from these types of foods.

Processed Foods *(cont.)*

Closing

1. Have the students keep a food diary for one day. You may wish to do this in class. If so, have them think about what they ate today for breakfast and lunch. Encourage the students to remember what they ate for dinner the night before.

2. Have the students describe and/or illustrate their food choices.

3. Ask the students to share with a partner in what ways their food was *processed*. Remind the students that many processed foods are still healthful to eat, such as apples that have been cooked to make applesauce. Encourage them to select one food and describe its main *ingredient(s)*, as well as any *additive(s)*.

4. Encourage the students to set one or more healthful food goals for the following day.

Extension

Have the students find magazine pictures or draw and color pictures of favorite foods. Ask, "How can you have that food in a less processed way?" For example, if students' favorite food is pizza, they can work with family members to make pizza at home. If they have pre-made pizza, they might have just one slice and have fruit or vegetables with it.

ELL Tip

Have the students work with a native speaking partner to identify and label food items during the Closing activity. Encourage the students to write at least one English word for each food item, for example, *sandwich* or *cereal*.

Play Dough

- 2 cups flour
- $\frac{1}{2}$ cup salt
- 1 tablespoon cream of tartar
- 1 teaspoon oil
- $\frac{3}{4}$ cup hot water

1. Stir dry ingredients together. Add oil.

2. Pour in water all at once.

3. Knead dough as necessary for consistency.

 # New Kinds of Plastic

Objective: Given articles expressing opposing viewpoints concerning biodegradable plastic, the students will complete a diagram to depict both views, and write a journal entry to reflect their own opinions.

Vocabulary

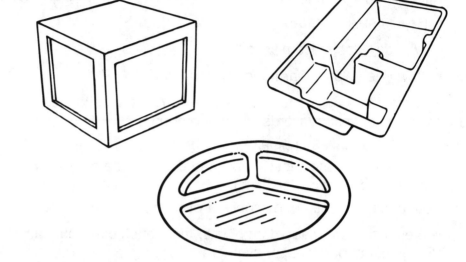

- allergen
- biodegradable
- biomass
- bioplastic
- contaminate
- emission
- fossil fuel
- methane
- pellet
- toxic

Materials

- Thinking About Bioplastics graphic organizer on page 36
- Statement FOR Bioplastics (reading level 7.6) on page 37 (one per student)
- Statement AGAINST Bioplastics (reading level 6.9) on page 38 (one per student)
- resources describing different technologies for making plastic (see Technology Resources on page 89)
- 10 index cards for each student (eco-friendlier option: use pieces of scrap paper)
- student dictionaries
- glue sticks and scissors
- word processing software (optional)
- Glossary on pages 92–96 (optional)

Preparation

Copy the graphic organizer and articles for each student (eco-friendlier option: scan into a document for student use or post on a class blog or Web page).

Opening

1. Distribute 10 index cards to each student.
2. Have the students prepare sets of word cards using the vocabulary words. Direct the students to write each word on one side of the card and its definition on the other side or create a set of cards using the glossary. Simply cut the word and definition strips, fold the cards, and glue them back-to-back.
3. Instruct the students to place their word cards in a stack with the word side faceup.
4. Have the students hold the cards, with one word facing out, and find a partner. Each student in the pair will define the other person's word.
5. Give the class time to find different partners to review as many definitions as possible.

 # New Kinds of Plastic (cont.)

Part 1

1. Divide the students into groups of three to five students.

2. Assign each group a question. More than one group may discuss the same question.
   - How is plastic made?
   - Why do people use plastic?
   - How does plastic harm the environment?

3. Have a class discussion to share students' responses to the questions. Encourage them to use new vocabulary words when appropriate.

4. Ask the class if anyone has heard of alternative forms of plastic or similar substances that are not made using fossil fuels and do not pose as great a threat to the environment. (biodegradable plastic, bioplastic)

5. Introduce the students to the concept of *bioplastics* and explain the process:
   - Bioplastics are made from plants, most often corn, but can also be made from sugarcane, potatoes, or even grass.
   - Plant matter is converted to polylactic acid (PLA).
   - PLA is used to make plastic pellets, which are molded to form plastic items.

Part 2

1. Give each student a Thinking About Bioplastics graphic organizer.

2. Tell the students they will read two articles expressing opposing viewpoints about new types of plastic. Distribute the articles, or assign reading the scanned Word documents or a class blog.

3. Explain that once the students have read both articles, they will complete the graphic organizer. On one side, they will write specific advantages of bioplastics. On the other side, they will list the disadvantages.

Thinking About Bioplastics	
Advantages	**Disadvantages**
Producing plastic from biomass results in fewer carbon emissions.	When bioplastics break down, they release methane gas.
Plastic made from plant matter is biodegradable.	Most recycling centers are not set up to recycle bioplastics.

New Kinds of Plastic *(cont.)*

Part 3

1. Have the students or groups research specific products made using biodegradable plastic, such as eating utensils and some food containers.

2. Invite each student or group to share one product with the class and what they learned about it.

Closing

1. Have the students reflect on their reading and research, and write a journal entry to express their own opinions about which would be better for the environment: to use biodegradable plastic or to refuse plastic altogether.

2. Discuss environmentally friendly options, such as using products that have already been recycled once and are therefore easier to recycle, or reusing items.

3. If time allows, hold a debate based on student responses to the plastics question.

Extension

Have the students research different technologies for biodegradable plastic and the benefits and drawbacks for each.

ELL Tip

Work with a small group to read the articles. Have the students follow along as you read aloud or have them participate in choral reading. Assist the students as they complete the graphic organizer by encouraging them to write simple words to describe each type of plastic.

Thinking About Bioplastics

Advantages	Disadvantages

New Kinds of Plastic *(cont.)*

Statement FOR Bioplastics

Bioplastics use biomass (plant matter), a renewable resource. Some people claim this type of plastic takes less energy to produce. As technology improves, it becomes more cost effective to produce bioplastics. Producing plastic from biomass results in fewer carbon emissions. The plastic is made from renewable (plant) sources instead of fossil fuels. This enables us to be less dependent on domestic and foreign oil.

Plastic made from plant matter, such as vegetable oil and cornstarch, is biodegradable. It is also non-toxic. The lack of chemicals enables it to break down more quickly. When it breaks down, it does not release harmful chemicals into the soil. Since it is made of natural materials, it is allergen-free. The production process removes any potential allergens from the corn or sweetness from the sugarcane.

PLA is the main substance in bioplastic. The consistency is like plastic. Many items can be made from it. It tolerates heat to 120°F, which is within the range of most common uses. It is freezer safe.

It can be recycled, although not with other plastic. Bioplastic can also be composted in a commercial facility. Scientists will research to learn if the methane gas released could be an alternate source of energy.

New Kinds of Plastic *(cont.)*

Statement AGAINST Bioplastics

Many scientists question how much energy and water it takes to produce bioplastic. Some people believe it takes more energy to produce plastic that will break down.

Growing the corn takes agricultural land and water resources. This land could be used to grow food. Farmers apply chemicals and pesticides to crops grown for industrial use. This may contaminate our food supply.

Most bioplastics need to be composted in a commercial composting plant. To break down, bioplastics require high levels of heat for a period of time. They need other specific things not usually found in backyard composting. A landfill may not have the proper conditions. Bioplastics need oxygen and enough heat or light to break down quickly.

When bioplastics break down, they release methane gas. This may harm the atmosphere more than carbon dioxide. Methane gas traps Earth's heat radiation more than carbon dioxide.

Bioplastics have a low melting point and can only be heated to 120°F. This means if a container made of this material sits in a car on a hot day, it may melt. It also cannot be microwaved.

Most recycling centers are not set up for PLA. It has to be sorted and separated from other types of plastic for recycling.

The Paperless Debate

Objective: Given a question-and-answer discussion, the students will brainstorm, prepare, and debate the advantages and disadvantages of going paperless in the classroom.

Vocabulary

- back up
- blog
- data
- debate
- flash drive
- PDA
- PDF
- paperless
- scanner
- surge
- wiki

Materials

- Going Paperless chart on page 43
- This Argument Makes Sense Worksheets on page 44
- Glossary on pages 92–96
- overhead projector, chart paper, or interactive whiteboard and appropriate markers
- strips of cardstock, large enough to display a sentence
- scrap paper (eco-friendlier option: individual whiteboards for each student and appropriate markers)
- resources about going paperless (See the Technology Resources on page 90.)
- pictures and other information about alternate processes of making paper (optional)
- access to slide presentation software or poster cards and markers (optional)

Preparation

1. Write one vocabulary word definition on each piece of cardstock or scrap paper. Do not include the actual vocabulary word. Write large enough for a classroom display. As an alternative, have the students write definitions on cards prior to the day of the lesson, or enlarge and copy each of the 11 definitions from the glossary onto cardstock.
2. Post the vocabulary word definitions around the classroom.
3. Edit the This Argument Makes Sense worksheet based on each group's speaking skills.
4. Copy and cut out a This Argument Makes Sense worksheet for each student.
5. Prepare the Going Paperless chart for class display by scanning it into an interactive whiteboard or preparing an overhead transparency. Enlarge as needed.

 The Paperless Debate *(cont.)*

Opening

1. List the vocabulary words on the board. Direct the students to review the words by copying each word on scrap paper or an individual whiteboard. Then have them locate the definition for each word posted in the classroom and write that definition next to each vocabulary word.

2. Call on students randomly to read each vocabulary word and state the location of the definition. Then have the students read the definition of the word.

3. Ask the students how these words might relate to each other. Many of the words refer to technology.

Part 1

1. Ask the students to take a few moments and imagine a classroom without paper. Invite the students to recall the opening vocabulary activity to help them brainstorm ideas. Begin a class discussion with the following questions:

   - How would teachers present information?
   - How would students learn new facts and concepts?
   - What would students read? What would they learn?
   - How would students complete assignments?
   - What would students do to show what they have learned?
   - How would students apply their learning?
   - How would parents know what goes on in the classroom?
   - How would parents be notified about important school information?

2. Draw a T-chart on the board. Label the left column, "Uses for Paper" and the right column, "Paperless Options."

3. Have the students list all the ways they use paper in class.

4. Then, list ways each task could be accomplished without using paper.

5. Guide the class discussion as necessary with the following thoughts and ideas:

   - assignments could be posted on a class Web site or blog
   - students could turn in assignments via e-mail or on flash drive
   - some items, such as permission forms or registration forms, may still need to be on paper

6. Invite the students to think of other ways in which they use paper at school. (paper towels, paper napkins)

7. Have the students brainstorm paperless options for these items. (cloth rags for wiping surfaces, packing a cloth napkin in their lunch)

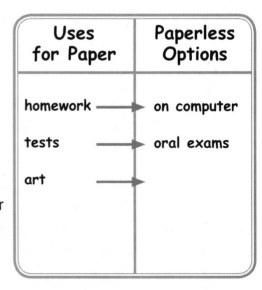

Uses for Paper	Paperless Options
homework ——→	on computer
tests ——→	oral exams
art ——→	

 The Paperless Debate *(cont.)*

Part 2

1. Refer to any technological options listed in the right column of the T-chart created in Part 1. Ask the students to consider the value of doing work online versus doing handwritten assignments.

2. Discuss how using technology helps or harms the environment.

3. Ask, "What are some environmentally friendly ways to use (paperless) technology?" (using a computer that has solar panels to recharge the battery)

4. Have the students research additional resources on going paperless as available. Discuss ways to have "the best of both worlds."

Part 3

1. Tell the students they will prepare to participate in a debate. Explain that when two groups with opposing views discuss an issue, it is called a *debate*.
   Review the basic rules for a debate:
   - Be respectful of one another's opinions.
   - Speak calmly.
   - Each member of the team should have an opportunity to speak and share his or her viewpoint.
   - Each team should take turns speaking.

2. Divide the class into four teams. Assign two teams the position of going paperless, taking the position that schools should use no paper. Assign the other two teams the position *against* going paperless. They will argue that schools still need to use paper for some things. **Note:** It might be helpful to remind the students that they do not have to agree with the team whose points they are presenting, only to present those arguments in a convincing manner.

3. Have each team compile notes from class discussions and add personal opinions to prepare to present their argument.

4. Conduct the debates. Have two teams debate their positions. The remaining two teams will be the audience.

5. Distribute copies of the This Argument Makes Sense worksheets to students. Have the students in the audience evaluate the debate as they listen.

6. Repeat for the second set of teams.

7. Write the names of the members of each debate team.

8. Circle the number that indicates the team's performance for each category. Circle one for "not very well" and five for "very well."

9. Add comments where appropriate.

Observer: _____

Debate Position: _____

Team Members: _____ _____
_____ _____

Directions: Circle the number that applies.

	Needs Work			Very Good	
Address the question	1	2	3	4	5
State your position	1	2	3	4	5
Defend your argument	1	2	3	4	5
Use facts and resources to make your points	1	2	3	4	5
Present debate in a logical manner	1	2	3	4	5
Participate in the debate	1	2	3	4	5

The Paperless Debate *(cont.)*

Part 4

1. Display the Going Paperless chart on an interactive whiteboard or overhead.
2. Invite the students to add advantages and disadvantages to the chart.
3. Review points from the students' debates to summarize the advantages and disadvantages of going paperless.
4. Determine what the class might do to address the points made.

Closing

1. Ask the students which paperless suggestions might work for their school.
2. Have the students write a letter to administrators, persuading them to consider implementing a few of these changes to help the school use less paper. The students should provide reasons for their position.

Extension

Divide the students into groups of three to five students each. Have each group research one of the following alternate methods of making paper:

- *hemp*—a plant whose fibers are used to make rope and sacks
- *kenaf*—a tropical plant, of the mallow family, yielding a fiber resembling jute; the fiber is used for cordage and textiles
- *bamboo*—a tropical plant with a hard, hollow stem, often used for making furniture and floors
- *papyrus*—a tall water plant that grows in northern Africa and southern Europe; paper is made from the stems of this plant

Direct each group to prepare a slide presentation (using computer software or poster cards) to tell the class about another method to make paper. Encourage the students to consider the following questions in their presentation:

- How does this method help or harm the environment?
- In what ways would this method of making paper be better than not using paper? Why?
- In what ways would this method of making paper be a valid alternative to the way paper is commonly made (using wood pulp)?

ELL Tip

Have native speakers help the students compile their notes and prepare their statements for the debate. The students may write and read one or two simple statements for their participation in the debate.

 # The Paperless Debate *(cont.)*

Going Paperless

Advantages of Going Paperless	Disadvantages of Going Paperless
✿ saves trees, which provide oxygen	✿ need more computers
✿ better for environment	✿ energy required for technology
✿ easy to manage data	✿ cost factor
✿ more organized learning	✿ need to back up data
✿ parents have direct access to information (instead of relying on students to convey the information)	✿ power surges
✿ material can be backed up to avoid the loss that can occur with lost paper copies	✿ computer problems

 # The Paperless Debate *(cont.)*

This Argument Makes Sense

Observer: _____

Debate Position: _____

Team Members: _____ _____

_____ _____

Directions: Circle the number that applies.

	Needs Work			Very Good	
Address the question	1	2	3	4	5
State your position	1	2	3	4	5
Defend your argument	1	2	3	4	5
Use facts and resources to make your points	1	2	3	4	5
Present debate in a logical manner	1	2	3	4	5
Participate in the debate	1	2	3	4	5

Comments:

- -

This Argument Makes Sense

Observer: _____

Debate Position: _____

Team Members: _____ _____

_____ _____

Directions: Circle the number that applies.

	Needs Work			Very Good	
Address the question	1	2	3	4	5
State your position	1	2	3	4	5
Defend your argument	1	2	3	4	5
Use facts and resources to make your points	1	2	3	4	5
Present debate in a logical manner	1	2	3	4	5
Participate in the debate	1	2	3	4	5

Comments:

A Green Lunch

Objective: Given a question-and-answer format, the students will generate a list of attributes for an environmentally friendly lunch and use those attributes as criteria to evaluate their own lunches.

> **Note:** This lesson should be taught before lunch.

Vocabulary

- environmentally friendly
- bulk
- pesticide

Materials

- Environmentally Friendly Lunches on page 48
- Lunch Analysis chart on page 49
- overhead projector, chart paper, or interactive whiteboard and appropriate markers
- sample lunch for each group (optional)

Preparation

1. Copy the Lunch Analysis chart for each group.
2. Review the suggestions listed on Environmentally Friendly Lunches prior to the lesson.
3. Prepare a sample lunch for each group. (optional)

Opening

1. Write the phrase *environmentally friendly* on the whiteboard or overhead projector. Draw a circle around the phrase to begin a brainstorming web.
2. Ask the students what they know about this phrase. If necessary, use the following prompts:
   - What does *environmentally friendly* mean?
   - What makes something environmentally friendly?
   - How could a student's lunch be environmentally friendly?
3. Introduce the remaining vocabulary by relating the words to the opening discussion. Ask the students how the words *bulk* and *pesticide* might relate to the concept of being environmentally friendly. Define the words as necessary.
   - People can buy foods in *bulk*, or larger quantities, to save on packaging.
   - A *pesticide* can be used to kill insects that might harm food crops, but some of these chemicals are also harmful to humans and the environment.
4. Ask the students how these words might relate to what they eat for lunch.

A Green Lunch *(cont.)*

Part 1

1. Use the brainstorming web, based on the students' prior knowledge, to generate a list of attributes for an environmentally friendly lunch. For example, an environmentally friendly lunch might include the following items:

   - reusable storage containers
   - foods purchased in bulk
   - fresh foods purchased locally
   - organic foods grown without pesticides or other chemicals
   - a thermos for hot foods or leftovers
   - reusable drink container
   - reusable silverware
   - cloth napkin

Part 2

1. Divide the class into groups of three or four students.

2. Distribute copies of Lunch Analysis to each group.

3. Have the students analyze one or more lunches to determine which items make use of reusable storage containers and which items would be thrown away, and how those items could be reduced, reused, or recycled. In the final column, indicate which items would end up in the trash, and later the landfill.

4. Direct the students to place check marks and explanations in the appropriate columns for each item in the lunch being analyzed.

Lunch Analysis

Food item/ Container	Reuse	Recycle	Reduce	Trash/landfill
sandwich in reusable container	✔ container			
unwrapped apple			✔ apple core goes in compost pile	
chips				✔ chip bag
bottle of water		✔ plastic bottle		

Teacher Note: You may wish to demonstrate how to fill in the Lunch Analysis chart with your own lunch prior to having the students break off into groups.

A Green Lunch *(cont.)*

Closing

1. Encourage the students to consider the attributes of an environmentally friendly lunch discussed in class. Remind the students to consider if any items in their lunches have been purchased in bulk and packaged in reusable storage containers.

2. Have the students rate their own lunches on a scale of 1 to 10, with 1 being "not at all" environmentally friendly and 10 being "very environmentally friendly."

3. Have each student write a paragraph evaluating his or her lunch.

Extension

Have the students create a pie graph to show the percentage of items in student lunches that are reusable, recyclable, or trash. Have the students create another graph a week later to show how any percentages have changed. Compare and discuss any differences between the two graphs.

ELL Tip

Work with a small group of students to help them complete the Lunch Analysis activity in Part 2. Discuss one or more examples to help the students understand how to describe a lunch item in each column of the grid.

Environmentally Friendly Lunches

- Encourage students to participate in packing their own lunches.

- Include reusable juice/water bottles.

- Consider using reusable silverware.

- Use cloth napkins instead of paper napkins.

- Buy in bulk and then place food items in smaller reusable containers.

- Buy fresh produce. Allow students to choose produce they like to eat.

- Buy local produce if possible.

- Read labels. Think twice about eating an ingredient that is difficult to read or pronounce—it is probably a chemical.

- Resist marketing and advertising ploys.

- Reduce the amount of packaged foods purchased.

- Consider making homemade items (cookies, muffins, trail mix, applesauce) and packing them in reusable containers. Make them on the weekend and freeze them for use during the school week.

- Many grocery stores also have a bakery for smaller quantities of baked items—check with the store in your area and bring your own bag.

- Buy organic food items to refuse or reduce the amount of chemicals used to grow foods.

- Maintain a class garden. Check with the school first. Use containers (if a garden plot is not available) to grow vegetables for lunches.

- Incorporate an area for composting lunch leftovers, lawn clippings, and leaves.

 # A Green Lunch *(cont.)*

1. List each item from your lunch and the type of storage container in the first column.

2. Determine what part of each item can be reused, recycled, or would reduce the amount of trash generated.

3. Check the appropriate rows for each item. Explain as needed. For example, if you brought a sandwich in a reusable container and an unwrapped apple in a reusable lunch bag, you would fill in the following columns; the rest would be blank:

   • **Food Item/Container**—sandwich in reusable container; unwrapped apple; reusable lunch bag

   • **Reuse**—containers; lunch bag

   • **Reduce**—apple core can go in the compost pile

Lunch Analysis

 # Is This Really Trash?

Objective: Given a question and a challenge, the students will think of new uses for old items and demonstrate their ideas to the class.

Vocabulary

- repurpose
- rethink

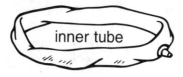

old towel

Materials

- Friend of Earth World Map on page 52
- overhead projector, chart paper, or interactive whiteboard and appropriate markers
- items that can be repurposed (e.g., bits of bar soap, plastic canister, molded plastic packaging, old towel, bike inner tube)
- index cards (eco-friendlier option: scrap pieces of cardstock)

Preparation

1. Prepare to play a variation of "Hangman" to introduce the two new vocabulary words on an overhead or interactive whiteboard. Copy the Friend of Earth World Map onto an overhead transparency.
2. Using the picture of Earth as the body. Explain that a body part will be added for each correct letter suggested. Make seven spaces for the word *rethink* and nine spaces for the word *repurpose* below the Earth.

Opening

1. Introduce the Friend of Earth game to the students. Explain that they will play a variation of "Hangman," taking turns calling out letters to fill in the blanks to spell two new vocabulary words. If a student guesses a letter that appears in the vocabulary words, you will add a body part to create a Friend of Earth person.

2. Continue having the students take turns until all the letters have been filled in for each new vocabulary word.

3. Once the words have been discovered, ask the students what they think the words *repurpose* and *rethink* mean. Assist the students with definitions as necessary.

Part 1

1. List the following items, which people throw away, on the overhead or whiteboard:

   - piece of eraser
   - paper
   - used gift card
   - plastic wrap
   - sock
   - empty chip bag
   - salsa jar and lid
   - cracked ink pen

2. Conduct a class discussion and add items to the list, based on student interest.

3. Ask the students which items on the list are really trash and which could be reused or *repurposed*. For example, clean plastic from packaging can be reused or repurposed as packaging to mail something or as a "brush" for art projects.

4. Place a check mark by items that might be repurposed to reduce the amount of trash going to the landfill.

5. Suggest to the students that to truly reduce trash, people need to learn to think differently. We should start to question, or *rethink*, what we throw away.

Is This Really Trash? *(cont.)*

Part 2

1. Show the students three or four items, such as bits of bar soap, a plastic canister from a bulk food item (e.g., pretzels, condiments, licorice), or molded plastic packaging from a toy or electronic product such as an MP3 player.

2. Challenge the students to think of ways to reuse these items and/or other items they might throw away.

3. Direct the students to present their ideas for new uses for the items.

4. Have the students write "product descriptions" on index cards for the repurposed items. Encourage the students to include the following features:

   - what the item looks like
   - what it does
   - the material(s) it is made from
   - who might use this product
   - how much they might pay for it
   - where such an item might be sold

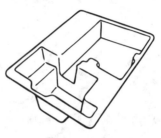

5. Display the items and their explanations.

Closing

1. Review the vocabulary words. Invite one or two students to explain the meanings of *repurpose* and *rethink*.

2. Divide the class into two teams. Give each team an item that could be repurposed— plastic container, old towel, sheet of printer paper, bike inner tube, etc.

3. Challenge each team to brainstorm ways to reuse the item.

4. Then have each team present its ideas. For instance, a student might say, "I reused a plastic container by putting part of my lunch in it." Or "I reused printer paper by taking notes on the blank side for my report."

Extension

Hold a debate about when reusing an item might not be a good idea. For example, reusing plastic resealable bags that had food stored in them might not be sanitary for the next use unless you can get the bag clean and dry. One group could take the position that it is always a good idea to reuse an item; the other group could argue that it is not always the best idea to reuse an item. Each group should give specific examples to back up their argument.

ELL Tip

Have the students work with a native speaking partner to discuss how to reuse items from the class-generated list in Part 1.

 Is This Really Trash? (cont.)

Friend of Earth World Map

52

 # Earth Fashion

Objective: Given suggestions and examples, the students will design a new use for a used article of clothing.

Note: This lesson may take more than one day to complete.

Vocabulary
- textile
- adhesive

Materials

- What to Do With Your Recycled . . . miniposter on page 55
- used clothing (e.g., pants, sweater, shirt)
- any materials students need to reuse their article of clothing (e.g., adhesive, scissors)
- markers, colored pencils, or crayons
- drawing paper
- Technology Resources on page 90
- rope and clothespins (optional)
- yarn or tapestry needle and yarn (optional)
- duct tape (optional)

Preparation
1. Have the students bring an article of used clothing to class. Or have them think of an example and draw a picture of that item.
2. Create a makeshift clothesline in the classroom using rope and clothespins to display the student drawings.
3. Plan to have extra used clothing on hand for the students who are unable to bring items to class.
4. Read the What to Do with Your Recycled . . . miniposter to become familiar with ways to repurpose used clothing prior to the lesson.

Opening
1. Discuss what determines fashion. (what people want and need; family, friends, and the media influence what we decide to wear)
2. A *textile* is a type of cloth or woven fabric. Explain that the textile industry offers recycling options for clothing that cannot be reused in other ways. (See Technology Resources on page 90 for more information on the environmental impact of clothing.)

 # Earth Fashion *(cont.)*

Part 1

1. Discuss ways to reuse or repurpose used clothing. (See the What to Do With Your Recycled . . . miniposter.) Hold up a used shirt, sweater, or pair of jeans. Sleeves can be cut off a used shirt and used as rags or cleaning cloths, and the shirt could be a smock for crafts. Jeans can be cut to make shorts, a skirt, or a purse.

2. Explain that clothing can be cut apart and the fabric can be reused in a variety of ways. For example, duct tape comes in many colors and provides a sturdy *adhesive* (a substance that holds things together). Fabric and duct tape can be used together to create new items.

3. Use one specific example discussed in class. Ask the students the following questions to help them brainstorm new ideas for the used item:

   - How would you personalize this idea?
   - How could you use this idea with a different article of clothing?
   - In what other ways could you reuse this item?

4. Have student volunteers offer ideas. After the first person has suggested an idea, encourage other students to use the original idea, as well as the new idea, to brainstorm other ideas.

Part 2

1. Have the students work together in pairs or small groups to brainstorm ways in which they could reuse an item of used clothing.

2. Ask the students to take specific notes or draw how they would reuse the item.

3. Provide time and materials for the students to repurpose the used clothing.

Closing

1. Conduct a "fashion show." Ask the students to hold up, model, or demonstrate their reused articles of clothing. Or have the students draw pictures of the new items and clip pictures to a clothesline across the classroom or display them on a bulletin board.

2. Ask the students how their reused clothing might become a new fashion. Have the students share what, if anything, they used as an adhesive to reconstruct their article of clothing.

3. Discuss what makes textiles so easy to recycle.

Extension

Demonstrate to the students how to loop yarn through fabric to close the bottoms of bags, pillows, etc. Use yarn and a yarn or tapestry needle. Discuss what additional new products might be made if sewing was an option.

ELL Tip

Invite the students to share ways people in their culture reuse clothing. Encourage them to include factors that affect how people use clothing such as climate, traditions, beliefs, values, and behaviors.

Earth Fashion *(cont.)*

What to Do With Your Recycled...

Jeans

- cut off legs and close for bags or purses
- use the top portion with pockets, cut off legs, close bottom opening, and thread a rope or a necktie through the belt loops for a drawstring on a bag or purse
- make lunch bags, potholders, or reusable grocery bags
- make chair pillows or cover an old chair
- use the pockets (with back fabric still attached) to make a pocket purse or potholder
- pin the pockets (with back fabric still attached) to a cork board and use as a pen or pencil holder

T-shirts

- cut up and put together T-shirts as a quilt (e.g., basketball team shirts, shirts from tournaments)
- cut off sleeves and collar, close bottom edge, insert pillow form and close top edge to create a pillow

Button-down Shirts

- use to make paint smocks or garden work shirts

Sweaters

- unravel sweaters with holes and use the yarn for other projects

Miscellaneous Clothing

- use smaller pieces of fabric for quilting, napkins, or rags
- cut old clothing into strips to braid to make a rug
- use strips of fabric as ties to stake garden plants
- use fabric from old clothing to cover photo albums or binders, or to make book covers

The Recycling Process

Objective: Given resources on recycling, the students will learn about the process of recycling and create a poster depicting the steps in the correct order.

Vocabulary
- recyclable
- aluminum
- ferrous

Materials
- small pieces of scrap paper
- Glossary on pages 92–96
- resources on the process of recycling (e.g., books, pamphlets from community, technology resources)
- overhead projector, interactive whiteboard, or chart paper and appropriate marker
- poster board and appropriate markers
- several common classroom items (e.g., CD, loose paper, textbook, glass science beaker, ruler, spiral bound notebook)

Preparation
1. Gather resources on the process of recycling and several common classroom items.
2. Write the lesson vocabulary words on the board.

Opening
1. Refer to the Glossary to read the definition for each lesson vocabulary word to the class.
2. Have the students write questions on scrap paper using each vocabulary word.
3. Direct the students to trade their paper with a partner and answer each other's questions. The students should write their answers using complete sentences.
4. Display miscellaneous classroom items (e.g., CD, textbook, ruler). Have the students consider which items might be recyclable and why.
5. Create a class chart on the overhead or whiteboard with student input. Label one column *Recyclable* and one column *Non-recyclable*. Have volunteers write suggested items in the correct columns.
6. Some items, such as tires, can be recycled, but often are not. Discuss with students how they might do additional research to see if tires, batteries, and other items might be recycled with a little additional effort.

The Recycling Process *(cont.)*

Part 1

1. Review the concept of "recyclable." Remind the students that even though an item is made of material that *can* be recycled, it may not be recycled in every community. For example, not all community recycling programs take certain forms of plastic.

2. Divide the students into groups for each category of recycling: paper, glass, cardboard, aluminum, ferrous metals, and non-ferrous metals.

3. Provide time and materials for each group to research the assigned recycling process.

4. Have each group of students create a poster showing the steps to recycle an item in the category they researched. Encourage the students to incorporate the lesson vocabulary where appropriate.

Part 2

1. Provide local community resources, such as brochures and specific Web sites, for the students to research recycling options in their community.

2. As a class, select one available process people may not commonly use.

3. Have the students create brochures for local recycling resources for that process.

Closing

1. Have the groups present their posters and brochures.

2. Encourage the students to share any specific information they learned related to the Opening discussion about items that are or are not recyclable.

Extension

Present the information and brochures to family members and others in the school and community at a Family Night or Open House.

ELL Tip

Work with a small group to research one recycling process. Assist the students in understanding and describing the process by using simple terms and visuals.

Electronic Landfill

Objective: Given examples of electronic devices commonly thrown away, the students will research options for reusing or recycling these electronic devices and write a report for peers.

Note: Plan ahead for this unit by collecting old CDs, MP3 players, computers, cell phones, etc.

Vocabulary

- E-waste
- electronic
- device
- upgrade

Materials

- old electronic devices (e.g., computers, cell phones, CDs, MP3 players)
- local community resources for disposal of electronic waste in your area (e.g., brochures, information from local waste management company)
- small pieces of scrap paper

Preparation

1. Research available options for safely disposing of electronic waste in your area (e.g., charity organizations, manufacturers) or have the students research the available options.
2. Check with others throughout the school and "rescue" electronic waste, such as a broken electric pencil sharpener, a cracked or "dead" CD that can no longer receive data, an MP3 player that someone replaced with a newer model, or a cell phone from someone who upgraded his or her phone.
3. Send an e-mail home to students, asking them to bring an electronic device they plan to throw away.
4. Have the students check with friends or family members for other old electronic devices.

Opening

1. Have the students discuss what makes something *electronic*. (It is powered by tiny amounts of electricity produced by electrons. Transistors, silicon chips, or valves control the electric current.)
2. Ask what it means to *upgrade* an electronic item. (To upgrade a product is to replace it with a better, more powerful, or recently released version.)
3. Ask why we call something electronic a *device*. (It does a particular job or fulfills a specific purpose.)
4. Explain how the term *E-waste* applies to electronic devices. (E-waste refers to electronic waste or garbage: electronic devices that get thrown away.)

 # Electronic Landfill (cont.)

Part 1

1. Ask the students to recall the last (personal) electronic device they replaced, either because it broke or they upgraded and got a new one.

2. Have the students write on a piece of scrap paper three things about their experience:
   - name of the electronic item
   - why they replaced it
   - what they did with the old electronic item

3. Instruct the students to turn and share their responses with a partner.

Part 2

1. Have the class create a pile with all the electronic trash collected.

   Safety Note: Check to make certain there are no leaking batteries or other chemical hazards.

2. Ask for the students' observations:
   - size of pile
   - number of electronic items
   - how many items, if any, would break down in a landfill
   - how much space this would take up in a landfill
   - estimate how many devices students in the community throw away each day

3. Have each student select one item from the pile. If necessary, a pair of students may work together with one item.

4. Invite the students to think of ways their item could be "rescued" to not become E-waste. Remind them to consider how the item could be reused (i.e., old computers for job training; scrap metal).

 # Electronic Landfill *(cont.)*

Closing

1. Direct the students to research and learn more about reusing and recycling E-waste.
2. The students may select one device and write a one-page report advising peers what to do with this type of used device instead of throwing it away.
3. Encourage the students to use the lesson vocabulary words correctly in their report.
4. Assist the students with documenting their research sources as necessary.

Extension

Challenge the students to conduct an E-waste drive to collect electronics that classmates, friends, parents, or other adults plan to throw away. Schedule a pickup with a reputable organization or organize a field trip to deliver the objects to a recovery facility in your area.

ELL Tip

Scaffold the students' discussion in Part 2 by giving specific examples of how electronic items can be reused or recycled:

- Many organizations take cell phones for recycling.
- MP3 players may be donated to charitable organizations or to a repair facility and then used by others.
- Many stores selling printer ink cartridges take them back for recycling or to refill with ink.
- Some manufacturers have computer "take-back" programs to recycle computers.

 # Recycle Your Lunch

Objective: Given an introduction to vocabulary and an article to read, the students will create and label a diagram, and write a plan describing how the composting process could be implemented on a classroom or school-wide basis.

Note: Use this lesson before "Grow Your Own Lunch" on pages 64–67.

Vocabulary

- compost
- microorganism
- decompose
- aerobic
- anaerobic
- aerate
- carbon
- nitrogen
- gray water

Materials

- How to Compost article (reading level 7.3) on page 63 (eco-friendlier option: scan into Word document, class blog, or interactive whiteboard)
- scrap paper (eco-friendlier option: individual student whiteboards or interactive whiteboard and appropriate markers)
- Glossary on pages 92–96

How to Compost

Composting occurs when microorganisms break down organic matter into topsoil. A compost pile requires air, water, and rotting material.

A compost pile can be aerobic or anaerobic. Aerobic compost relies on organisms that require oxygen. It takes more work, but less time to acquire compost. Turn this type of pile on a regular basis to aerate the compost. Anaerobic compost has organisms that do not require as much oxygen. These heaps have a higher nitrogen content and tend to be dark and slimy.

The ratio of material should be 3:1 carbon (dry/brown) to nitrogen (wet/green). Dry leaves, dry grass clippings, wood ash, and plain paper (including food-related paper, such as untreated paper towels and napkins) contain carbon. Add nitrogen to the heap by including fresh grass clippings, garden weeds, fruit and vegetable peels, lettuce leaves, coffee grounds, and tea bags. Do not add meat, dairy products or pet waste to the pile—this may attract rodents.

Compost materials decompose faster if you break items into smaller pieces. For example, crush eggshells or shred bits of paper or lettuce leaves.

A compost pile needs some water. Keep it just moist enough to hold together, but not so wet that water will squeeze out of it. It is okay to use "gray water" as long as any detergents are environmentally friendly. A shovel full of garden soil will help get the process started.

Composting can also be accomplished on a small scale using worms. Some people call this vermi-composting. Use red worms instead of earthworms. Line a small covered bin with shredded newspaper or plain paper, shredded leaves or straw. Add worms and food scraps. Monitor the process and do not add food scraps in greater amounts than the worms can handle.

When you can use your compost depends on how quickly the materials have broken down. An aerobic pile that receives oxygen from frequent turnings has bacteria and organisms that break down matter quickly. Compost may be ready to harvest in a few weeks or a few months, depending on the weather. A nutrient-rich anaerobic pile takes longer to mature as the organisms in that pile work more slowly. In colder winter months, the composting process may cease almost completely.

You will be able to tell when you have some compost ready to harvest. It will no longer look like the original materials, but rather like dirt. When you harvest your compost, you can use it in a garden as mulch around bedding plants or on the lawn. You can also use compost in potted plants or in a container garden.

Preparation

1. Have on hand the definition for each lesson vocabulary word to read during the Opening activity. (See the Glossary on pages 92–96.)
2. Prepare the How to Compost article for student reading, one copy for each student or display the article for the whole class.

Opening

1. Introduce the lesson vocabulary by playing a game of tic-tac-toe. Have students draw a tic-tac-toe grid on a piece of scrap paper or an individual whiteboard. (Or play the game as a whole group using an interactive whiteboard.)
2. List the vocabulary words on the board. Direct the students to write one word in each space on their tic-tac-toe grid in random order.
3. Read the definition for each vocabulary word. Students will write an X over that word on their grid.
4. When a student has three Xs in a row, he or she will stand, read each word, and restate the definition.

Recycle Your Lunch *(cont.)*

Part 1

1. Ask the students which garbage can is the largest in their house. (most likely the kitchen garbage can)
2. Have the students draw a box on their scrap paper or whiteboards to represent a garbage can.
3. Ask them to draw a line to indicate how much of the garbage can gets filled with food scraps. (Research indicates 25–30% of our solid waste consists of food scraps and yard trimmings.)
4. Explain that many food scraps are organic and could be recycled to make compost. Meat and dairy should not be composted. Fruits and vegetables, coffee grounds, and egg shells can be composted.

Part 2

1. Divide the students into groups. Ensure that each student or group has a copy of the How to Compost article or display the article on an interactive whiteboard for the whole class.
2. After the students read the selection, have them draw a diagram explaining the process of making compost.
3. Direct the students to include labels on their diagrams.
4. Suggest that they list items to include in a compost pile.

Closing

1. Display one or more student diagrams (block out names if desired). As you discuss the process of composting, point out how each vocabulary word relates.
2. Have the students write a plan describing how they could compost lunch scraps and yard trimmings from the school grounds. Encourage them to correctly use lesson vocabulary words in their writing.

Extension

Have the students work together as a class to compile their ideas for a composting plan for the classroom or school. If appropriate, submit the plan to administrators. Have the class work with others in the school, such as cafeteria workers, maintenance personnel, and administration, to put into practice the student-generated composting plan.

ELL Tip

Assist the students as they read the How to Compost selection. Stop at each vocabulary word and review the meaning. Help the students rephrase the sentences in simpler terms to aid comprehension.

How to Compost

Composting occurs when microorganisms break down organic matter into topsoil. A compost pile requires air, water, and rotting material.

A compost pile can be aerobic or anaerobic. Aerobic compost relies on organisms that require oxygen. It takes more work, but less time, to acquire compost. Turn this type of pile on a regular basis to aerate the compost. Anaerobic compost has organisms that do not require as much oxygen. These heaps have a higher nitrogen content and tend to be dark and slimy.

The ratio of material should be 3:1 carbon (dry/brown) to nitrogen (wet/green). Dry leaves, dry grass clippings, wood ash, and plain paper (including food-related paper, such as untreated paper towels and napkins) contain carbon. Add nitrogen to the heap by including fresh grass clippings, garden weeds, fruit and vegetable peels, lettuce leaves, coffee grounds, and tea bags. Do not add meat, dairy products, or pet waste to the pile—this may attract rodents.

Compost materials decompose faster if you break items into smaller pieces. For example, crush eggshells or shred bits of paper or lettuce leaves.

A compost pile needs some water. Keep it just moist enough to hold together, but not so wet that water will squeeze out of it. It is okay to use "gray water" as long as any detergents are environmentally friendly. A shovel full of garden soil will help get the process started.

Composting can also be accomplished on a small scale using worms. Some people call this vermi-composting. Use red worms instead of earthworms. Line a small covered bin with shredded newspaper or plain paper, shredded leaves or straw. Add worms and food scraps. Monitor the process and do not add food scraps in greater amounts than the worms can handle.

When you can use your compost depends on how quickly the materials have broken down. An aerobic pile that receives oxygen from frequent turnings has bacteria and organisms that break down matter quickly. Compost may be ready to harvest in a few weeks or a few months, depending on the weather. A nutrient-rich anaerobic pile takes longer to mature as the organisms in that pile work more slowly. In colder winter months, the composting process may cease almost completely.

You will be able to tell when you have some compost ready to harvest. It will no longer look like the original materials, but rather like dirt. When you harvest your compost, you can use it in a garden as mulch around bedding plants or on the lawn. You can also use compost in potted plants or in a container garden.

 # Grow Your Own Lunch

Objective

Given a brainstorming session and small group discussion, the students will plan, create, and maintain a container garden.

Note: Use this lesson after "Recycle Your Lunch" on pages 61–63.

Vocabulary

- container
- drainage

Materials

- Container Gardens on page 67
- Technology Resources on page 90
- overhead projector, chart paper, or interactive whiteboard and appropriate marker
- sheet of white paper for each student
- magazine and seed catalogs, featuring pictures of gardens
- large containers—planters, pots, plastic tubs (eco-friendlier option: old containers that are not in use; reuse containers such as milk jugs with narrow top cut off)
- compost from "Recycle Your Lunch" lesson, if available
- soil, or inexpensive garden or potting soil
- vegetable seeds, sprouts, or donated plants
- hammer and nail and rocks or gravel, if containers do not have holes

Preparation

1. Arrange to get used containers and soil from the school maintenance department or as donations. Try local businesses, too.
2. Check ahead of time for permission and possible locations to have a container garden at school. Some resources listed in the Technology Resources indicate that some plants may be successfully grown indoors, if necessary.
3. Collect pictures of gardens and seed catalogs to research sources for seeds, sprouts, and plants.

Opening

1. Introduce the word *container* as used in the context of a garden. Explain that in this lesson, the students will need to use containers (e.g., plastic jar or container) that are big enough to hold a plant.
2. Invite students to brainstorm types of containers they could reuse as planters, such as milk jugs, old buckets or cracked trash cans, large bulk tubs in which school supplies were purchased, etc.
3. Introduce the word *drainage* by explaining that the students will need to put holes for drainage in their chosen containers if holes are not already there. They will be using a hammer and nail to make the holes in the container. *Drainage* holes allow excess water to escape so the plant roots will not rot. (Adult supervision is suggested.)
4. Write the word *garden* on the board or post a single word card so the class can read it. Display magazine or catalog pictures of gardens.
5. Generate a class list on the board or overhead transparency of various fruits and vegetables the class could grow in a container garden. (See Container Gardens on page 67.)
6. Encourage the students to add pictures of gardens to the board or other display area. Use these as guides or inspiration when planning the class garden layout.

Grow Your Own Lunch *(cont.)*

Part 1

1. Give each student a sheet of white paper. Ask them to create a web using the word *garden* in the center. Have the students complete the web by brainstorming items they would like to grow in a container garden to eat.

2. Have the students write a journal entry about why a container garden might be a good idea. Encourage them to consider what they learned in the lessons "Processed Foods" and "Recycle Your Lunch." They may also discuss why they included certain items on their web.

3. Divide the students into small groups. Ask the students to share their journal entries and ideas for a container garden.

4. Have each group create survey questions to ask other class members about container gardens. Refer to the sample survey questions below, if necessary.

5. Allow time for the students to ask the survey questions.

6. Have the groups share the survey results with the class.

7. Determine which plants the students would like to grow and where. Remind the students to take into account the area in which they live, the season, and the materials available. Be realistic. A few healthy plants growing in the right conditions will go a long way to show the students that they can grow food!

Part 2

1. If possible, have the students research the Web sites listed in Technology Resources to learn more about container gardening. Explain that they will be planning a garden for their class or school and need to pick plants that will do well in the climate, with the available light in the area they will be using.

2. Discuss the amount of light their plants will need. Determine the best way to arrange the containers so plants will receive the right amount of light.

3. Continue to discuss various factors to consider such as those listed on the Container Gardens page.

4. Map out a class plan for the garden's layout.

5. Create a T-chart on the overhead or whiteboard, listing the benefits and drawbacks to container gardening.

Sample Survey Questions

- Why should our class have a container garden?
- Where would be the best place to put a container garden?
- Would you rather grow carrots or peas?
- Should we include fruits? Why or why not?
- Do you want to grow lettuce and tomatoes or just tomatoes?
- What should we do with the harvest from our garden?

Grow Your Own Lunch *(cont.)*

Part 3

1. Work together as a class or in small groups to determine group roles such as

   - preparing containers and soil
   - harvesting/gathering compost, if used
   - planting seeds, sprouts, or donated plants
   - watering and checking the water needs of the plant
   - weeding and insect watch and removal

2. Have the students plant the containers and label each one with the date planted, care required, and expected date for "harvest."

3. Work with the students to maintain the class container garden and record its progress.

Closing

1. As a class, revisit the T-chart, listing the benefits and drawbacks to container gardening. Ask the students what they might do differently next time.

2. Apply the lesson vocabulary words, *container* and *drainage*, to the discussion as appropriate.

Extensions

1. Have the students prepare a presentation about container gardening and present it to another class or community group.

2. Challenge the students to try planting seeds in the container garden using vegetables they eat at home, such as bell peppers, tomatoes, or dried peas.

ELL Tip

Pair each student with another student who is more proficient in English when writing the journal entries. List content-related words on the board, such as *container*, *drainage,* or specific names of vegetables, to help the students with their writing.

 # Grow Your Own Lunch *(cont.)*

Container Gardens

Plants for Container Gardens

- blueberries
- beans
- broccoli
- carrots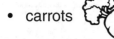
- celery
- cucumbers
- dwarf lemon tree

- eggplant
- garlic
- grapes
- greens
- herbs
- lettuce
- onions

- orange
- peas
- peppers
- potatoes
- raspberries
- strawberries
- tomatoes

Container Gardening Tips

- Containers will need adequate drainage—holes and/or a 1–2" layer of small rock/gravel. Have the students punch holes with pencil points in cardboard or plastic containers.

- Use a pot large enough for each plant's root ball.

- Plan for enough room for plant growth.

- Remember that soil in pots dries out faster than in the ground—if possible, choose plants that require less water.

- If necessary, consider containers made of materials that are frost-safe.

- If pots will need to be moved occasionally, make sure they are not too heavy or cumbersome. Or enlist help to construct one or two simple dollies with a piece of board with four casters mounted on the underside of the wood.

- Plastic pots will work for container gardens.

- If possible, use a potting soil mix.

- Make certain that drainage will not damage the area. If necessary, add trays and/or rocks under the pots.

Conserve Natural Resources

Objective: Given various reference materials, the students will research ways to conserve our natural resources and will present their findings to the class.

> **Note:** This lesson may take more than one day to complete.

Vocabulary

- conserve
- degrade
- erosion
- filter
- mulch
- natural resource
- nutrient
- pollutant
- reservoir
- timber
- urban
- virgin
- wetland

Wetlands

    Wetlands describe areas where water meets land. Water is at or near the surface of the soil. Wetlands occur along coastal areas, rivers, and streams, and in the middle of prairies. Cattails and other plants that live in water thrive in wetlands.

    Some wetlands have water only part of the year. But they still provide habitats for plants and animals. Many endangered or threatened species live in wetland areas. Wetlands also filter nutrients and pollutants out of water. They help reduce flooding of rivers.

    Urban development threatens wetlands. People fill in the wetland area to build houses, highways, and airports on the land. Wetlands have even been used for landfill sites. Pollution degrades the quality of wetland waters.

    Pond and lake development often results in draining or flooding wetlands. The resulting reservoirs provide water for recreation. They may prevent flooding of other land. However, they destroy natural ecosystems.

    Students can work together to help protect wetlands in their area. Become aware of any pollution that may impact a local wetland. Pick up litter. Try to identify the source of trash affecting the wetland.

    Students can help raise awareness of the importance of and danger to wetlands. Consider signing up for a local Trash Pickup Day to clean a wetland area.

Materials

- Precious Water article (reading level 7.5) on page 70
- Save Our Trees article (reading level 6.5) on page 71
- Wetlands article (reading level 6.9) on page 72
- Technology Resources on page 90
- available reference materials about conservation of natural resources
- 8" x 10" piece of poster board, cardstock, or light-colored cardboard for each group
- whiteboard, chart paper, or overhead projector
- small pieces of scrap paper
- Glossary on pages 92–96

Preparation

1. Make a copy of one of the reading articles for each group member.
2. List the vocabulary words on the whiteboard, chart paper, or overhead projector.

Opening

1. Read the definition for *natural resources* from the Glossary. Have the students brainstorm and generate a class list of natural resources. (water; wood or timber; fuel, such as natural gas or oil; metals, such as iron or copper; plants; animals)
2. Read the definition for *conserve* from the Glossary. Ask the students to write one suggestion on a piece of scrap paper for how people can conserve natural resources.
3. Have the students turn and share their suggestion with a partner.
4. Ask the students to write sentences with the remaining lesson vocabulary words, leaving out the vocabulary word and drawing a blank line instead.
5. Direct students to trade papers with a partner and fill in the appropriate vocabulary words.

Conserve Natural Resources *(cont.)*

Part 1

1. Assign the students to small groups and hand out the articles. Each group will focus on one natural resource. (There may be more than one group reading each article.)

2. Have the students research their natural resources. The students may read the appropriate article provided, use technology resources listed, or read any additional, approved materials available.

3. Each group will prepare a miniposter on an 8" x 10" piece of poster board, describing how to conserve their natural resource and use it wisely. On the back of the miniposter, they should draw a picture depicting their natural resource (i.e., a river if their resource is water).

4. Group members will determine a location in the classroom in which to display their miniposter. They will write clues about their resource for other classmates to find their miniposter.

5. Have the group write their resource and location on a card to turn in, along with their natural resource miniposter and clues.

Part 2

1. At a time when students are out of the room, display the miniposters around the classroom with the picture side facing out.

2. Give each group the clues written by another group. Have the students use the clues to find that natural resource card.

Closing

1. Ask each group to share how to conserve the natural resource listed on the miniposter they located.

2. Review the lesson vocabulary words by having the students from each group discuss the words in the context of their specific article.

Extension

Have the students use what they have learned about conserving natural resources to create a coloring book for younger students. Each page should have a drawing and one or two simple sentences that describe that resource.

ELL Tip

Divide the students into small groups of three, with an ELL student who is more proficient in English and a native speaker, to read the article in Part 1. Have the students highlight difficult words as they read. Encourage more proficient students to help explain concepts using simple drawings and terms from the students' primary languages.

Conserve Natural Resources *(cont.)*

Precious Water

Three-quarters of Earth is covered with water. Only a small percentage of that is fresh water that is suitable for human use. With more people living on Earth every year, water has become a valuable resource.

People can conserve water by collecting rainwater. They can use the water for household tasks, such as watering plants and cleaning. Some cities allow people to flush toilets with stored rainwater.

Water-efficient toilets or showerheads also help conserve water. Families can install water-saving showerheads or faucet aerators. Fixing leaky faucets or toilets is another way to save water.

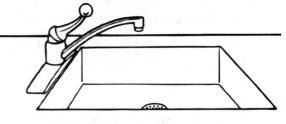

Conserve water by turning off a faucet when it is not being used. For example, turn off the water while brushing your teeth or washing hands with soap. Do not run a faucet waiting for water to become cold enough to drink. Instead, fill a pitcher with tap water and keep it in the refrigerator. People can also take shorter showers or use less water in the bathtub.

Some tasks people use water for can be completed without water. For example, sweep a driveway to clean it instead of rinsing it with a hose. A layer of mulch around plants will reduce evaporation, and the plants will not need to be watered as often.

Conserve Natural Resources *(cont.)*

Save Our Trees

Forests provide people with renewable resources. People use wood for fuel and timber for building. They make paper and other products from trees. Sustainable forest programs seek to use trees wisely. It is important not to use forests faster than new trees can be planted and grown.

Many people recycle paper. Try to purchase products made with recycled paper. Paper can be saved by using both sides. When printing a computer document, set the printer to print on both sides of the page. Use recycled paper whenever you can. Submit assignments online if possible.

Many things we purchase have paper packaging. Look for items that have reduced packaging. Consider cloth or reusable substitutes for paper goods such as paper plates, napkins, or cups.

Planting trees helps the environment in several ways. Trees contribute oxygen to the atmosphere. They remove carbon dioxide and other chemicals from the air. Tree roots help prevent soil erosion and keep waterways cleaner.

Trees provide shelter from the elements. A more extensive tree cover would reduce the amount of energy needed to heat and cool buildings. Trees also block the wind, reducing the need for heating and cooling. This reduces the need for power plants.

Trees and other plants can create a calm environment. Forests also provide homes for many plants and animals.

Conserve Natural Resources *(cont.)*

Wetlands

Wetlands describe areas where water meets land. Water is at or near the surface of the soil. Wetlands occur along coastal areas, rivers, and streams, and in the middle of prairies. Cattails and other plants that live in water thrive in wetlands.

Some wetlands have water only part of the year. But they still provide habitats for plants and animals. Many endangered or threatened species live in wetland areas. Wetlands also filter nutrients and pollutants out of water. They help reduce flooding of rivers.

Urban development threatens wetlands. People fill in the wetland area to build houses, highways, and airports on the land. Wetlands have even been used for landfill sites. Pollution degrades the quality of wetland waters.

Pond and lake development often result in draining or flooding wetlands. The resulting reservoirs provide water for recreation. They may prevent flooding of other land. However, they destroy natural ecosystems.

Students can work together to help protect wetlands in their area. Become aware of any pollution that may impact a local wetland. Pick up litter. Try to identify the source of trash affecting the wetland.

Students can help raise awareness of the importance of wetlands and danger to them. Consider signing up for a local Trash Pickup Day to help clean a wetland area.

Greener Cleaners

Objective: Given information about environmentally friendly cleaning ingredients, the students will test various ingredients in the classroom and compare them with untreated surfaces for effectiveness.

Vocabulary

- vinegar
- borax
- castile soap
- eucalyptus

Materials

- Greener Cleaners on pages 75–76
- Technology Resources on page 90
- clean rags
- surfaces to clean; if necessary, use sample floor tiles or carpet squares
- sample Green cleaning ingredients (e.g., baking soda, lemon juice, white vinegar, borax, essential oils, liquid castile soap)
- bowls, measuring and mixing tools
- access to a binding machine or another way to compile a class book (optional)

Preparation

1. Identify possible surfaces in the classroom for the students to clean, such as door knobs, a corner of a windowpane, student desks or table tops, coat hooks, countertops, keyboards, etc.
2. Check any existing regulations or guidelines in place for your school or district regarding cleaning items in classrooms.
3. Gather the necessary cleaning ingredients (see Greener Cleaners), bowls, and mixing materials and supplies.
4. Make enough copies of the Greener Cleaners recipes, so each student in a small group has a copy of the group's assigned cleaner recipe.

Opening

1. Introduce or review with the students common abbreviations used in recipes, such as **tsp**. for teaspoon, **T.** for tablespoon, **c.** for cup, etc.
2. Introduce the non-chemical ingredients for cleaning using the following definitions:
   - *vinegar*—a sour liquid containing acetic acid, made by fermenting liquids, such as cider, wine, malt, etc.
   - *borax*—sodium borate, a white crystalline salt
   - *castile soap*— a fine, mild, hard soap prepared from olive oil and sodium hydroxide
   - *eucalyptus*—a tall, aromatic, evergreen tree found mainly in Australia from which an oil is extracted

Greener Cleaners *(cont.)*

Part 1

1. Divide the students into four or five groups.

2. Assign each group an ingredient and have them read the information and cleaner recipe pertaining to that ingredient. What do they think it is used for? What might it be used for to clean?

3. As a class, discuss possible surfaces within the classroom that the students can clean with their cleaning ingredients.

4. Create a list of possible surfaces.

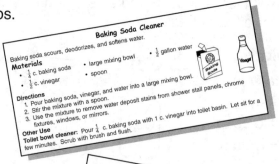

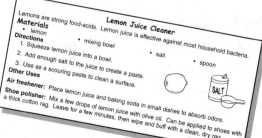

Part 2

1. Explain to the students that they will be using natural ingredients as cleaning products to test their effectiveness.

2. Distribute the necessary cleaning ingredients to the student groups. The students will use their ingredients, along with the information on their recipe card, to make a solution with which to clean a sample item or area.

3. Have each group use their ingredients to clean a specific item or area in the classroom.

4. Ask the students to write a few sentences describing the difference in appearance and cleanliness between the surface area they cleaned and the areas they did not clean.

5. Rate the products used. Which would they suggest using again?

Closing

1. Have the students present the results of their cleaning experience to the class.

2. Review reasons for establishing Green cleaning practices.

3. Review the lesson vocabulary: *vinegar, borax, castile soap, eucalyptus oil*. Have the students give at least one use for each ingredient.

Extensions

1. Invite the students to create a flyer or a "recipe" book to distribute to family members. Each group should write how they used their ingredients. Copy the pages and bind the "recipes" into a book for each student.

2. Have the students conduct further research using information from the Web sites in the Technology Resources.

ELL Tip

Work with a small group to read its assigned ingredient recipe card. Use pictures or diagrams to explain unfamiliar concepts.

 # Greener Cleaners *(cont.)*

Baking Soda Cleaner

Baking soda scours, deodorizes, and softens water.

Materials

- $\frac{1}{2}$ c. baking soda
- $\frac{1}{4}$ c. vinegar
- large mixing bowl
- spoon
- $\frac{1}{2}$ gallon water

Directions

1. Pour baking soda, vinegar, and water into a large mixing bowl.
2. Stir the mixture with a spoon.
3. Use the mixture to remove water deposit stains from shower stall panels, chrome fixtures, windows, or mirrors.

Other Use

Toilet bowl cleaner: Pour $\frac{1}{4}$ c. baking soda with 1 c. vinegar into toilet basin. Let sit for a few minutes. Scrub with brush and flush.

Lemon Juice Cleaner

Lemons are strong food-acids. Lemon juice is effective against most household bacteria.

Materials

- lemon
- mixing bowl
- salt
- spoon

Directions

1. Squeeze lemon juice into a bowl.
2. Add enough salt to the juice to create a paste.
3. Use as a scouring paste to clean a surface.

Other Uses

Air freshener: Place lemon juice and baking soda in small dishes to absorb odors.

Shoe polisher: Mix a few drops of lemon juice with olive oil. Can be applied to shoes with a thick cotton rag. Leave for a few minutes, then wipe and buff with a clean, dry rag.

White Vinegar Cleaner

Vinegar cuts through grease, removes mildew and stains, and kills viruses, germs, bacteria, and mold.

Materials

- $\frac{1}{4}$ c. white vinegar
- mixing bowl
- 4 c. club soda
- spoon

Directions

1. Pour white vinegar and club soda into a bowl.
2. Mix the solution with a spoon.
3. Use rags made from T-shirts or crumpled newspapers with the solution to clean a surface.

Other Uses

Lime and stain remover: Use full-strength white vinegar to clean lime or hard water stains.

Carpet cleaner: Mix $\frac{1}{4}$ c. each of white vinegar, salt, and borax to form a paste. Rub paste into carpet and leave for a few hours; then vacuum.

 # Greener Cleaners *(cont.)*

All-Purpose Cleaner

All-purpose cleaners are designed to clean many different types of washable surfaces including sinks, toilets, patio furniture, appliances, and stainless steel. They can also degrease, remove grime, deodorize, and disinfect other bathroom surfaces.

Materials

- 1 tsp. borax
- 1 tsp. baking soda
- 2 tsp. vinegar
- $\frac{1}{4}$ tsp. dish soap
- 1 tsp. fresh lemon juice
- 2 c. hot water
- mixing bowl
- spoon
- spray bottle

Directions

1. Pour borax, baking soda, vinegar, dish soap, lemon juice, and hot water into a bowl.
2. Mix the solution with a spoon.
3. Store in a spray bottle. Spray on floors or countertops to clean them.

Essential Oil Cleaner

Essential oils leave a pleasing smell, while cleaning at the same time! They remove toxic mold, stale air, unpleasant odors, and kill viruses, bacteria, and dust mites. **Note:** Find essential oils at health food or grocery stores.

Materials

- $1\frac{1}{2}$ c. water
- $\frac{1}{2}$ c. distilled white vinegar
- mixing bowl
- spoon
- 20 drops essential oil (e.g., tea-tree, lavender, eucalyptus)

Directions

1. Pour water, vinegar, and essential oil into a bowl.
2. Stir the solution with a spoon.
3. Soak a comb or brush for 20 minutes, rinse, and air dry.

Other Use

Furniture polish: Add a few drops of lemon oil to $\frac{1}{2}$ c. warm water. Mix well and store in a spray bottle. Spray the mixture onto a soft cotton cloth until slightly damp. Use the cloth to polish varnished wood furniture.

Castile Soap Cleaner

Castile soap is gentle enough for all skin types. It will clean almost anything, and it is biodegradable! Use castile soap to clean counters, bathrooms, and kitchen utensils.
Note: Find castile soap at grocery, natural food, or discount retail stores.

Materials

- 1 T. liquid castile soap
- mixing bowl and spoon
- $\frac{1}{3}$ c. baking soda

Directions

1. Pour soap and baking soda into a bowl.
2. Combine the mixture into a soft paste using a spoon.
3. Use the paste to scrub sinks or tile.

Other Uses

Floor cleaner: Mix 2 tsp. castile soap with 3 gallons hot water. Wipe the floor; then rinse with 1 c. vinegar mixed with 3 gallons cold water.

Produce cleaner: A couple of dashes in water cleans pesticide residues off fruits and vegetables.

Green Collar Jobs

Objective: Given "job postings" on a bulletin board, the students will read a job description for a job that interests them, research to learn more about that job, and write a business letter to a mock Human Resources department at a company.

Vocabulary

- industry
- proposal
- residential
- aerial
- renewable

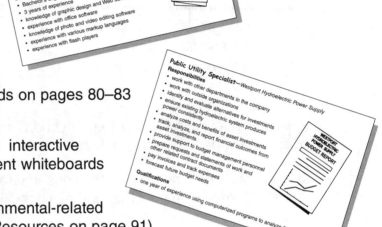

Materials

- Green Collar Sample Classified Ads on pages 80–83
- 4 sheets of cardstock
- scrap paper (eco-friendlier option: interactive whiteboard and/or individual student whiteboards and appropriate markers)
- additional resources about environmental-related industries and jobs (Technology Resources on page 91)
- access to word processing software for students to read information (optional)
- scanner (optional)

Preparation

1. Copy the Green Collar Sample Classified Ads onto cardstock and cut apart the job description cards.

2. Create a bulletin board display showcasing the job descriptions (eco-friendlier option: scan each job description into a word processing document, which will also enable more students at a time to access multiple description cards in a computer lab).

Opening

1. Share the new vocabulary: *industry, proposal, residential, aerial, renewable.* Use an interactive whiteboard to involve as many students as possible, or randomly select students to come to the board while the rest of the class follows along using scrap paper or individual whiteboards.

2. Call out the vocabulary words, one word at a time. Have the students write each word as creatively as possible using a variety of lettering styles.

3. Ask the class how they might group certain words. Use student observations to discuss the meanings of the vocabulary words.

4. If time allows, have the students write a few sentences using selected vocabulary words. Ask volunteers to read their sentences aloud.

 # Green Collar Jobs *(cont.)*

Part 1

1. Introduce the concept of "green collar jobs." Explain that green collar jobs are not exclusively jobs in which employees develop solar or wind power technology.

2. Draw two webs on the board to help the students brainstorm green collar jobs.

3. Use one web for positions that are "Green" in nature such as the following professions:

   - scientists
   - research technicians
   - engineers
   - solar panel installers
   - energy-efficient building architects
   - wind turbine manufacturers
   - urban planners
   - solar sales
   - renewable energy industries
   - alternative power industries (e.g., hybrid cars, solar panels, wind turbines, hydropower, geothermal and nuclear power, resource conservation)

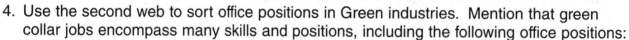

4. Use the second web to sort office positions in Green industries. Mention that green collar jobs encompass many skills and positions, including the following office positions:

   - analysts
   - managers
   - project leaders
   - administrators
   - communicators
   - information technicians (computer-related)
   - security personnel
   - clerical/administrative support

   Where on the web might students put these options?

   - bicycle repairers
   - reporters
   - teachers

5. Continue the discussion of green collar jobs by asking, "Why might you want to have a green collar job?"

   - reduce waste and pollution
   - benefit the environment
   - increase energy efficiency
   - change wasteful practices

6. Tell the students that many renewable energy industries are labor intensive, which provide more jobs. Many of these positions are "middle skill" level jobs, requiring a high school diploma plus some training. Not all the jobs require a college degree—at least not at entry level.

 # Green Collar Jobs *(cont.)*

Part 2

1. Introduce the job postings bulletin board. Explain that sometimes in college placement offices or other community career centers, available jobs are posted on a bulletin board for interested people to read. Most job postings contain the job responsibilities and requirements for the job.

2. Have the students read the postings and choose one that interests them. Explain that they will be writing a letter to the mock company, expressing interest in pursuing the career described. Review business letter format as needed.

3. Direct the students to think about the skills they would need to apply for the job and to think about what they could be doing now, or which classes they might take in the future, to start preparing for that career path.

4. The students may need to research the job further to find out whether or not they would be interested in pursuing steps needed to fulfill those requirements. For example, if a job posting in wetlands evaluation required a degree in biology, would they be willing to pursue the steps to obtain such a degree?

5. Instruct the students to write letters describing their interest in the position and what steps they plan to take to prepare for that career. Encourage them to use appropriate lesson vocabulary. The students may ask for advice or guidance as well.

Closing

1. Have the students interview each other to learn more about different green collar jobs.

2. The students may introduce their partner to the class using the information they learned in the interview process, if time allows.

3. Use the following questions to conduct a class discussion. Encourage the students to incorporate lesson vocabulary words in their answers.

   Which of these green collar jobs . . .

   - might we see in the near future in our community?
   - does our community need? Why?
   - most appeals to you? Why?
   - already exist in our community?

Extension

Hold a job fair. Group together two or three students with similar "jobs" to work at each booth. Have the students prepare a display to give information about their jobs. Invite parents to view the student displays.

ELL Tip

Work with a small group to assist the students as they read the Green Collar Classifieds. Paraphrase the reading in simple terms to aid student comprehension. Discuss responsibilities and qualifications as needed to assist student understanding.

Green Collar Jobs (cont.)

Sample Classified Ads

Web Developer—*Environmental Specialists, Inc.*

Responsibilities

- work as part of a team
- determine program needs and how to accomplish the task
- meet deadlines
- develop software—design, code, and test product
- ensure software meets standards
- communicate well with team and customers
- identify problems, recommend and implement solutions

Qualifications

- Bachelor's degree in Computer Science or Management Information Systems
- in place of the above degrees, have a technical degree (math/science) and computer experience
- 4–6 years of experience with database server software
- knowledge of SQL language
- experience with graphic design, video editing, and Web development software
- knowledge of good software engineering practices
- prefer project management experience

Senior Field Biologist—*Environmental Specialists, Inc.*

Responsibilities

- evaluate wetlands
- work within guidelines of the National Environmental Policy Act (NEPA)
- provide project management
- develop proposals
- assist with marketing

Qualifications

- Bachelor's degree in Biology or a water science degree related to geology
- prefer Master's degree
- 5 years of relevant experience
- excellent written and oral communication skills
- good word processing and spreadsheet skills

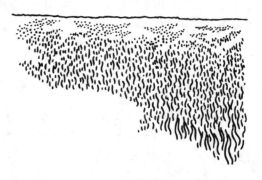

Green Collar Jobs *(cont.)*

Sample Classified Ads *(cont.)*

Graphic Artist—*Environment Laboratories, Inc.*

Responsibilities

- design graphics for print and/or Web use to support proposals, marketing, and technical publications
- create designs for public Web sites
- meet deadlines
- work on several projects at a time
- accept direction and critique and be willing to revise artwork

Qualifications

- Bachelor's degree in Graphic Design
- 3 years of experience
- knowledge of graphic design and Web development software
- experience with office software
- knowledge of photo and video editing software
- experience with various markup languages
- experience with flash players

Public Utility Specialist—*Westport Hydroelectric Power Supply*

Responsibilities

- work with other departments in the company
- work with outside organizations
- identify and evaluate alternatives for investments
- ensure existing hydroelectric system produces power consistently
- analyze costs and benefits of asset investments
- track, analyze, and report financial outcomes from asset investments
- provide support to budget management personnel
- prepare requests and statements of work and other related contract documents
- pay invoices and track expenses
- forecast future budget needs

Qualifications

- one year of experience using computerized programs to analyze financial data

 # Green Collar Jobs *(cont.)*

Sample Classified Ads *(cont.)*

Construction Manager—*SunPower Solar Installation Company*

Responsibilities

- manage residential solar power projects
- manage work crews and check for safety, quality, and efficiency
- work on project to install solar power as needed
- manage project resources (materials, tools and equipment, labor)
- interpret construction drawings
- work with project managers and engineers

Qualifications

- 5 years of experience in construction management
- knowledge of the National Electric Code, Uniform Building Code, and OSHA safety standards
- attention to detail with emphasis on quality and safety
- ability to travel and be onsite during project installation
- good oral and written communication skills
- strong work ethic
- organization and time management skills
- basic computer knowledge (word processing and spreadsheet software)

Software Development Engineer—*Renewable Energy Project Group, Inc.*

Responsibilities

- design, develop, and improve services
- help clients make decisions about renewable energy projects
- work as a team player
- work under limited supervision
- learn new systems and technologies quickly

Qualifications

- Bachelor's degree in Computer Science, Engineering, Earth Science, or equivalent experience
- excellent knowledge of programming languages
- experience working with operating systems
- excellent problem-solving abilities
- ability to meet deadlines
- commitment to good development practices
- interest in renewable energy and earth science
- experience working with large amounts of data
- knowledge of geospatial analysis tools

 # Green Collar Jobs (cont.)

Sample Classified Ads (cont.)

Executive Assistant—*Brinet Renewable Energy Systems*
Responsibilities
- maintain and organize the department leader's schedule and work flow
- direct phone calls and visitors
- use spreadsheet, word processing, and slide presentation software
- prepare executive papers, correspondence, and reports
- incorporate accounting and finance information into presentations and reports
- prioritize and manage the time lines of the department's projects and on-going work
- provide administrative support to the department
- assist others on special projects

Qualifications
- 5 years of experience as an administrative assistant, with 2 years at an executive level
- understanding of accounting and financial concepts
- good organizational and interpersonal skills
- excellent written and verbal communications skills
- proficient with word processing, spreadsheet, slide presentation, e-mail, and calendar management software
- ability to handle confidential information
- strong customer service focus
- attention to detail and accuracy

Helicopter Pilot—*Hydroelectric Power Resources*
Responsibilities
- perform pilot-in-command duties in a turbine-powered aircraft
- work with a mission crew (pilot, lineman, and/or mission equipment operator)
- perform aerial patrols of power lines
- perform aerial photography and surveys
- maintain crew coordination, communications, and situation awareness
- interpret weather reports
- determine safe routes to fly
- file flight plans
- perform contract services as required

Qualifications
At a minimum, applicants must have:
- commercial pilot certificate helicopter class and instrument ratings
- 1st or 2nd class FAA medical certificate
- minimum of 150 flight hours as pilot-in-command of turbine-powered helicopters in the last 12 months
- been assigned as a pilot-in-command under a FAA operation during the previous 2 years
- 2 years of flight experience as pilot-in-command in the utility industry, or 3 years of low-level flight activities in single engine turbine helicopters in mountainous terrain
- no pilot-error aircraft accidents or FAA violations in the previous 5 years
- total helicopter flying time of 2,500 hours

Enriching the Environment

Objective: Given a review of vocabulary words and concepts learned, the students will present their ideas about what students can do to help the environment to another group of students.

Vocabulary

Review all vocabulary words in the Glossary.

repurpose

to use for another reason or in another way

Materials

- Glossary vocabulary cards on pages 92–96
- What Students Can Do on pages 87–88
- recycled materials to make "tree" with "leaves" (e.g., cardboard, paper, brown paper bags, leaf-colored scrap paper)
- free-standing portable screen or large poster board
- overhead projector, interactive whiteboard, or chart paper and appropriate markers
- scissors
- access to slide presentation or word processing software (optional)
- public domain images or magazine pictures (optional)
- scanner (optional)

Preparation

1. Obtain permission and a date for the class to present what they have learned about enriching the environment to another class or at a school assembly.
2. Determine which vocabulary words, if not all, you wish to have the students review.
3. Copy the Glossary vocabulary cards, and have student volunteers cut them apart. You may wish to assign each student several words.
4. Gather and prepare equipment as needed for a group presentation.

Opening

1. Review the vocabulary words by having the class play a matching game similar to Concentration.

2. Use a set of word and definition cards for each game. Post the words and definitions facedown on the board or a wall, or lay them facedown on the floor.

3. Each student will take a turn flipping over two cards in an attempt to find a word card and its matching definition card. If the cards do not match, the student turns them back over and the next student takes a turn by flipping over two more cards.

4. Play as long as time allows or until all the vocabulary words have been matched with the correct definitions.

bulk		
	large quantities	

Enriching the Environment *(cont.)*

Part 1

1. Explain that the students will prepare a presentation for another group. Their presentation will consist of two parts: introducing words that relate to taking care of the environment, and practical things students can do to help the environment.

2. As a class, decide which words to introduce to the audience.

3. Have the students assemble a tree with recycled brown paper bags and leaf-colored scrap paper to cut leaves to surround the word cards. The students may mount the tree and leaves on a free-standing portable screen or a large poster board.

4. Instruct the students to create the word cards using selected vocabulary words. Each student will make a "leaf," and be prepared to tell what that word means.

5. Ask the students to prepare an introduction to explain how trees enrich the environment. Guide the students to include the following information about trees.

   - Trees provide oxygen in the atmosphere to help balance carbon footprints.

   - Trees are a renewable source of energy.

   - Tree roots hold soil, which prevents erosion and flooding.

   - Trees provide foods such as fruit and nuts.

   - Trees provide shelter for people, animals, and birds.

Part 2

1. Conduct a class discussion about making environmentally friendly choices. Ask the students what they have learned about helping the environment.

2. Take notes on the overhead or interactive whiteboard.

3. Display What Students Can Do, if desired. Encourage the students to add specific ideas from the lessons to each R word category (*Refuse, Reduce, Reuse, Recycle, Research, Respond*).

Enriching the Environment *(cont.)*

Part 3

1. Divide the students into six groups. Assign each group one R word category (*Refuse, Reduce, Reuse, Recycle, Research, Respond*).

2. Have the students create a presentation using slides or word processing software, an interactive whiteboard, overhead projector, or other medium. Each group's presentation will focus on what students can do to help the environment in that particular area.

3. Direct the students to refer to any class assignments and scan any drawings or pictures to illustrate their ideas.

Closing

1. Direct the students to gather all the information and materials necessary for their presentations.

2. Have the students give their presentations to another class or in a school assembly as planned.

Extension

If possible, have the students present their information in a community setting, such as an environmental education center or save student files (use initials or other coded names to protect student privacy) to a flash drive, and offer to donate the presentations to a local community education center. Have the students create and then set up a display with a three-dimensional tree, similar to the tree they created for their school presentation. Include environmental words and concepts in the display. Obtain permission to set up the display in a community education center.

ELL Tip

Have the students write one or two things they remember from the lessons before they meet with their group. Provide step-by-step instructions, as necessary, for the students as they work with their group to create slides for their presentation.

 # What Students Can Do

Refuse

Take a *reusable bag* to the store.
  Why?
  • Most plastic is made from fossil fuels.
  • Manufacturing plastic takes energy.

Reduce

Carpool to school and sports events.
  Why?
  • saves gasoline; gasoline uses energy
  • cuts down on air pollution and carbon dioxide emissions

Walk or *ride* a bike.
  Why?
  • does not produce air pollution and carbon dioxide emissions

Conserve water.
  Why?
  • Earth has a lot of water, but most of it is saltwater in the oceans.
  • There are many people on Earth; it takes a lot of water for people to live.

Reuse

Hand down *clothing*.
  Why?
  • More than one person can use an item.
  • Making new things takes energy.

Use reusable *cups*.
  Why?
  • Keeps garbage out of landfills.
  • Uses fewer products.

Use both sides of *paper*.
  Why?
  • Uses less paper.
  • Saves trees, a natural resource.

What Students Can Do *(cont.)*

Recycle

Recycle *paper*.
 Why?
- Keeps trash out of landfills.
- Saves trees and energy.

Recycle *aluminum cans* and *other metals*.
 Why?
- Keeps trash out of landfills.
- It takes less energy to recycle scrap metal than to mine and form new metal products.

Recycle *water*.
 Why?
- Water is a valuable resource.

Research

Learn about ways you can help the *environment*.
 Why?
- There are many things you can do to make the environment better.
- A clean environment is healthful for humans and animals.

Respond

Plant a *tree*.
 Why?
- Trees take in carbon dioxide and give oxygen back to the atmosphere.

Show someone how to *recycle items in your community*.
 Why?
- In many places, it is easy to recycle items and it keeps trash out of landfills.

Clean up playgrounds, parks, ball fields, school yards, and roadsides (with grownups).
 Why?
- Litter is harmful to plants and animals, and it is ugly.

Technology Resources

Think Green

It's Cool to Go Green

The Oregonian, Portland, Oregon, "Frugality Is Cool in Back-to-School Shopping"
http://www.oregonlive.com/business/index.ssf/2009/08/frugality_is_cool_in_backtosch.html

FOX 40 WICZ TV station, "Students Learn Going Green Is Cool"
http://www.wicz.com/news2005/viewarticle.asp?a=9568

My EcoExpress, "It's Cool to Be Green"
http://www.myecoexpress.com/news8.htm

Time for Kids, "A Mobile, Green Museum"
http://www.timeforkids.com/TFK/kids/news/story/0,28277,1891055,00.html

Time for Kids, "A Sneak Peek at the Smart Home"
http://www.timeforkids.com/TFK/kids/news/story/0,28277,1890235,00.html

National Geographic for Kids, Zipper's Green Tips
http://kids.nationalgeographic.com/Stories/SpaceScience/Green-tips/

Discovery Education, ThinkGreen
http://www.ThinkGreen.com/classroom

Carbon Footprints

Environmental Protection Agency Information on the Carbon Dioxide Cycle in the Atmosphere
http://www.epa.gov/climatechange/emissions/co2.html

Refuse

Processed Foods

"What Are Processed Foods?"
http://nutrition.about.com/od/askyournutritionist/f/processedfoods.htm

"How Products Are Made: Graham Cracker"
http://www.madehow.com/Volume-3/Graham-Cracker.html

New Kinds of Plastic

Food Service Warehouse, Restaurant Supplies and Equipment
"Plant versus Plastic: The Advantages of Biodegradable Disposables"
http://www.foodservicewarehouse.com/education/going-green/plant-vs-plastic.aspx

Green Living Tips, "Degradable, Biodegradable, Compostable"
http://www.greenlivingtips.com/articles/197/1/Degradable-Biodegradable-Compostable.html

Earth 911, "The Scoop on Bioplastics"
http://earth911.com/blog/2009/03/16/the-scoop-on-compostable-plastic/

 # Technology Resources *(cont.)*

Reduce

The Paperless Debate

Eminence Middle School, Kentucky

http://www.education-world.com/a_tech/tech059.shtml

http://www.paperlessclassroom.org/story.htm

http://www.paperlessclassroom.org/ktlc2003/ KTLCworkshop_files/frame.htm

West Blocton Elementary School, Alabama

http://www.abpc21.org/withoutpaper.html

Alternate methods of making paper

handmade paper (recycled paper)

http://www.pioneerthinking.com/makingpaper.html

kenaf paper

http://www.ecomall.com/greenshopping/kenafx.htm

hemp paper

http://www.ehow.com/how_4472282_make-hemp-paper.html

bamboo paper

Scroll down through the page to get to the section on how to make bamboo paper.

http://www.jmbamboo.com/bamboo_FAQ_information/ bamboo_uses.php

rice paper

http://www.rice-paper.com/about/makeyourown.html

Reuse

Earth Fashion

Council for Textile Recycling

http://www.textilerecycle.org/

Environmental impact of clothing

http://earth911.com/household/clothing-and-textile/ facts-about-clothes/

Recycle

The Recycling Process

Earth 911.com

http://www.Earth911.com

paper

http://www.gp.com/EducationalinNature/paper/ recycling.html

cardboard

http://www.corrugated.org/Recycling/ RecyclingProcess.aspx

glass

http://www.reachoutmichigan.org/funexperiments/ agesubject/lessons/newton/GlssRecycl.html

metal

www.Earth911.com/metal

Recycle *(cont.)*

Recycle Your Lunch

Introduction to composting—slide show

http://sustainable.tamu.edu/slidesets/kidscompost/ cover.html

Recipe for compost

http://www.ecy.wa.gov/programs/swfa/kidsPage/ compost.html

Composting tips

http://www.seventhgeneration.com/learn/news/ garbage-gold-how-compost-planet-profit

http://meetthegreens.pbskids.org/episode4/ kitchen-composting.html

Worm composting

http://www.msue.msu.edu/objects/content_revision/ download.cfm/item_id.207836/workspace_id.-30/ OC0355%20Worm%20Composting.pdf/

http://aces.nmsu.edu/pubs/_h/h-164.pdf

School composting program

http://planetgreen.discovery.com/work-connect/composting-program-kids-school.html

Recycling Facts—A Recycling Revolution— Closing the Loop

http://www.recycling-revolution.com/recycling-facts. html

Grow Your Own Lunch

Texas A & M Department of Horticultural Sciences, "Vegetable Gardening in Containers"

http://aggie-horticulture.tamu.edu/extension/container/ container.html

University of Arizona College of Agriculture & Life Sciences, "Vegetable Garden: Container Garden"

http://ag.arizona.edu/pubs/garden/mg/vegetable/ container.html

University of Illinois Extension, "Making Herb and Vegetable Containers"

http://urbanext.illinois.edu/containergardening/herb-veggie.cfm

Life on the Balcony, "Gardening Tips and Tricks for Apartment and Condo Dwellers"

http://lifeonthebalcony.com/category/ fruits-and-vegetables/

Technology Resources *(cont.)*

Research

Conserve Our Natural Resources

Water
WaterSense, U.S. Environmental Protection Agency
http://www.epa.gov/WaterSense/
Planet Green, "Using Stored Rainwater"
http://planetgreen.discovery.com/home-garden/stored-rainwater-waters-lawn.html

Forests
TreeLink, "Energy Efficiency"
http://www.treelink.org/linx/factoid.php
USDA Forest Service
http://www.naturalinquirer.org/about-usda-forest-service-v-18.html
Recycled paper
http://www.environmentalpaper.org/documents/Qand%20A.pdf
Recycled fiber
http://www.environmentalpaper.org/documents/recycledfiberfactsheet2.pdf
Endangered forests
http://www.environmentalpaper.org/documents/EF-overview.pdf

Wetlands
Wetlands Education, U.S. Environmental Protection Agency
http://www.epa.gov/owow/wetlands/education/
Natural Resources Conservation Service, Living in Harmony with Wetlands
http://www.nrcs.usda.gov/feature/highlights/wetlands/

Backyard Conservation
Natural Resources Conservation Service
http://www.nrcs.usda.gov/feature/backyard/
Wildlife Habitat Council, Teacher lesson page
http://www.wildlifehc.org/managementtools/backyard-lessonplans.cfm

General Conservation Resources
National Association of Conservation Districts
http://www.nacdnet.org/education/
National Wildlife Federation
http://www.nwf.org/

Research *(cont.)*

Greener Cleaners
How Stuff Works.com, "How Green Are Household Cleaners?"
http://home.howstuffworks.com/green-household-cleaners.htm
Green Living, "Castile Soap"
http://www.greenlivingtips.com/articles/221/1/Castile-soap.html
Natural Pesticides
http://www.allpestco.com/2009/05/natural-plant-deterents-for-roaches-and-silverfish/

Green Collar Jobs
American Solar Energy Society, GreenStart Job Board
http://www.ases.org/jobs
USA Jobs
http://jobsearch.usajobs.gov/

Respond

Natural Inquirer, Middle School Science Education Journal
http://www.naturalinquirer.org/
Recycling Process
http://www.mde.state.md.us/Programs/LandPrograms/Recycling/Education/process.asp
U.S. Environmental Protection Agency, Make a Difference Campaign
http://www.epa.gov/osw/education/mad.htm
Environmental Tips
http://www.ncenvirothon.org/CEI%202009/Talking%20Trash.pdf
http://planetgreen.discovery.com/

Note: Teachers may wish to locate specific articles and cut and paste into Word or HTML documents (on a blog) for student use as some advertisements may be inappropriate for younger students.

Glossary

additive	something that is added to a substance to change it in some way
adhesive	a substance, such as glue, that makes things stick together
aerate	to expose to air or cause air to circulate throughout
aerial	happening in the air
aerobic	able to live, grow, or take place only where free oxygen is present
allergen	a substance inducing an allergic state or reaction
aluminum	a light, silver-colored metal
anaerobic	able to live and grow where there is no air or free oxygen
back up	to duplicate a computer file or program as a precaution against failure
biodegradable	something that can be broken down naturally by bacteria
biomass	organic matter, especially plant matter, which can be converted to fuel; a potential energy source
bioplastic	plastic derived from renewable biomass sources, such as vegetable oil or cornstarch
blog	a Web log; an online diary
bulk	large quantities
carbon	a chemical element found in coal and diamonds and all plants and animals
carbon dioxide	a natural gas consisting of carbon and oxygen
carbon footprint	compares the human demand for resources with Earth's ability to regenerate or replenish those resources
chronological	arranged in the order in which events happened

compost	mixture of rotted leaves, manure, etc., added to soil to improve it
conserve	to save something from loss, decay, or waste; to preserve
consumer	someone who buys and uses products and services
container	a receptacle for holding goods
contaminate	to make unfit for use
data	information or facts
debate	a discussion between sides with different views; to consider or discuss something
decompose	to break up into parts by a chemical process
degrade	to lower or corrupt in quality
device	a piece of equipment that does a particular job
drainage	the act or process of draining
E-waste	electronic waste
efficient	works very well and does not waste time or energy
electronic	containing transistors, silicon chips, or valves that control an electric current
emission	substance discharged in the air
environmentally friendly	products made of substances that do not damage the natural environment and are reusable or can be recycled easily
erosion	the gradual wearing away of a substance by water or wind
ferrous	describes metal that contains or comes from iron, such as steel

 # Glossary  *(cont.)*

fiber	a long, thin thread of material such as cotton, wool, hemp, or nylon
filter	to clean liquids as they pass through it
flash drive	a small data storage device that plugs into the USB port of a computer
fossil fuel	coal, oil, or natural gas; formed from the remains of prehistoric plants and animals
gray water	dirty water from sinks, showers, bathtubs, washing machines, etc., which can be recycled
impact	the effect something has on a person or a thing
industry	manufacturing companies and businesses, taken together; a single branch of business or trade
ingredient	one of the things an item is made from
media	a means of communicating information to large numbers of people
methane	a colorless, odorless gas that burns easily and is used for fuel
microorganism	a living thing that is too small to be seen without a microscope
mulch	leaves, straw, peat moss, etc., spread on the ground around plants to prevent evaporation of water from the soil
natural resource	a material found in nature that is necessary or useful to people
nitrogen	a colorless, odorless gas that makes up about four-fifths of the earth's air
nutrient	something that is needed by people, animals, and plants to stay strong and healthy
organic	using only natural products and no chemicals or pesticides
paperless	without using paper
PDA	personal digital assistant; a hand-held computer often pen-based

 # Glossary *(cont.)*

PDF	portable document format or portable document file; can include any combination of text, graphics, and images
pellet	a small, spherical body
pesticide	chemical used to kill pests, such as insects
pollutant	anything that pollutes or contaminates
post-consumer	generated after someone buys a product or service (i.e., after someone has used an item)
pre-consumer	generated before someone buys a product or service (i.e., during the manufacturing process)
processed	used a series of steps to change it
proposal	a plan or idea
recycle	to process used items, such as glass, plastic, newspapers, and aluminum cans, so that they can be used to make new products
recyclable	material or object that can be recycled
reduce	to make something smaller or less
refuse	to say you will not do something or accept something
renewable	not depleted (as in energy sources); able to be renewed; does not take things away from the environment that cannot be put back
repurpose	to use for another reason or in another way
research	to study and find out about a subject, usually by reading many books about it or by doing experiments
reservoir	a natural or artificial holding area for storing a large amount of water
residential	having to do with a neighborhood or an area where people live

 # Glossary *(cont.)*

respond	to react to something
rethink	to question and learn to think differently about an object or situation
reuse	to use again instead of throwing something away
scanner	a machine that scans an image to be converted into a computer graphics file
surge	a sudden increase, as in power
sustainable	able to be kept going, as in resources that can continue to be used
synthetic	something that is manufactured or artificial, rather than found in nature
textile	a fabric or cloth that has been woven or knitted
timber	cut wood used for building; lumber
toxic	poisonous
trend	the general direction in which things are changing; the latest fashion
upgrade	to replace a computer part or a piece of software with a better, more powerful or more recently released version
urban	to do with or living in a city
virgin	untouched or in its natural state, as in virgin forests
waste	garbage, or something left over and not needed
wetland	marshy land; land where there is much moisture in the soil
wiki	a collaborative Web site; its content can be edited by anyone who has access to it